# Perrito
## para colorear

**Coloring Pages for Kids**



Coloring Pages for Kids
An imprint of Ciparum LLC

Perrito para colorear
© 2017 Ciparum LLC
All rights reserved.
ISBN-10:1-63589-537-5
ISBN-13:978-1-63589-537-7

**Coloring Pages for Kids**

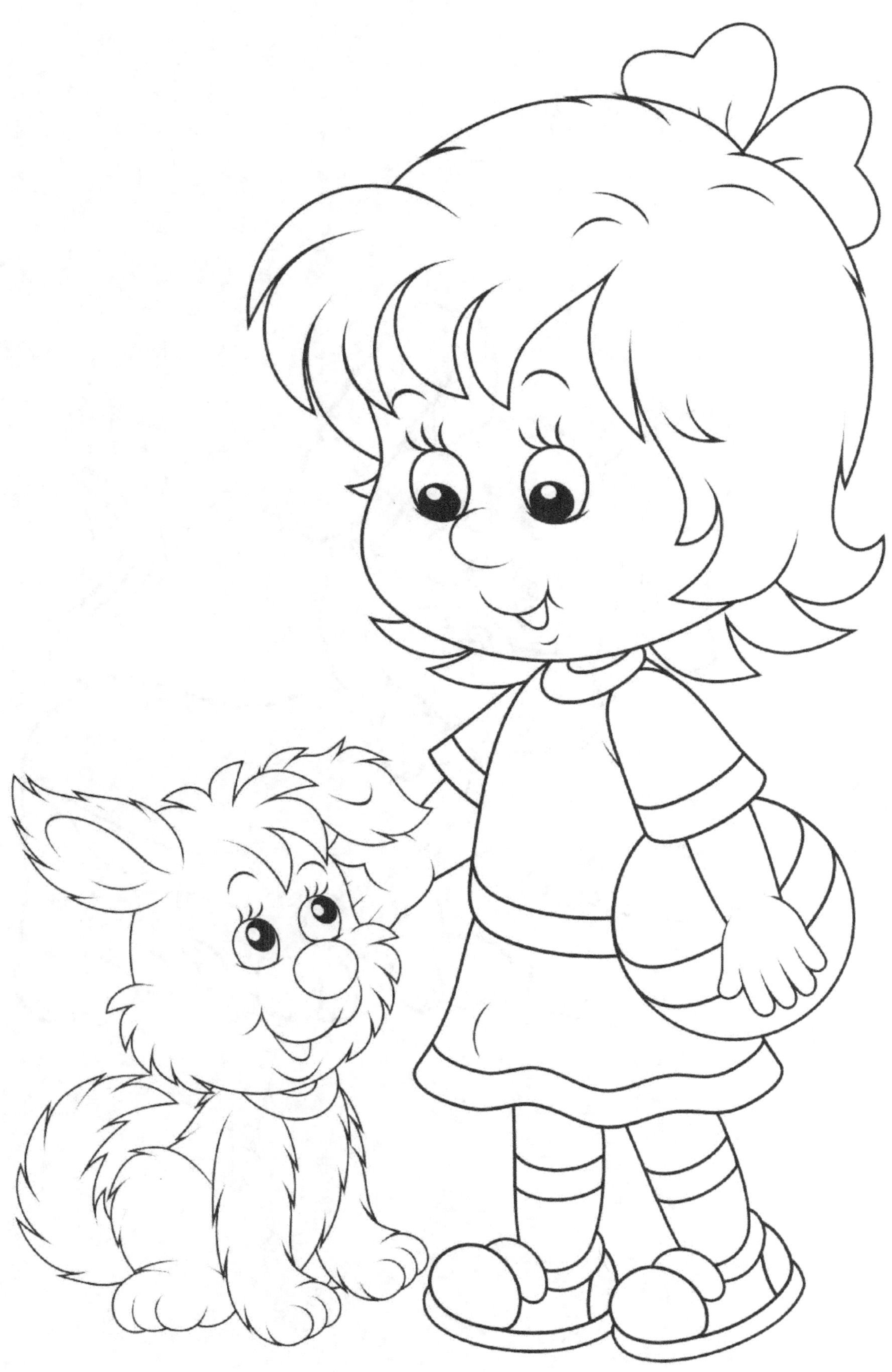

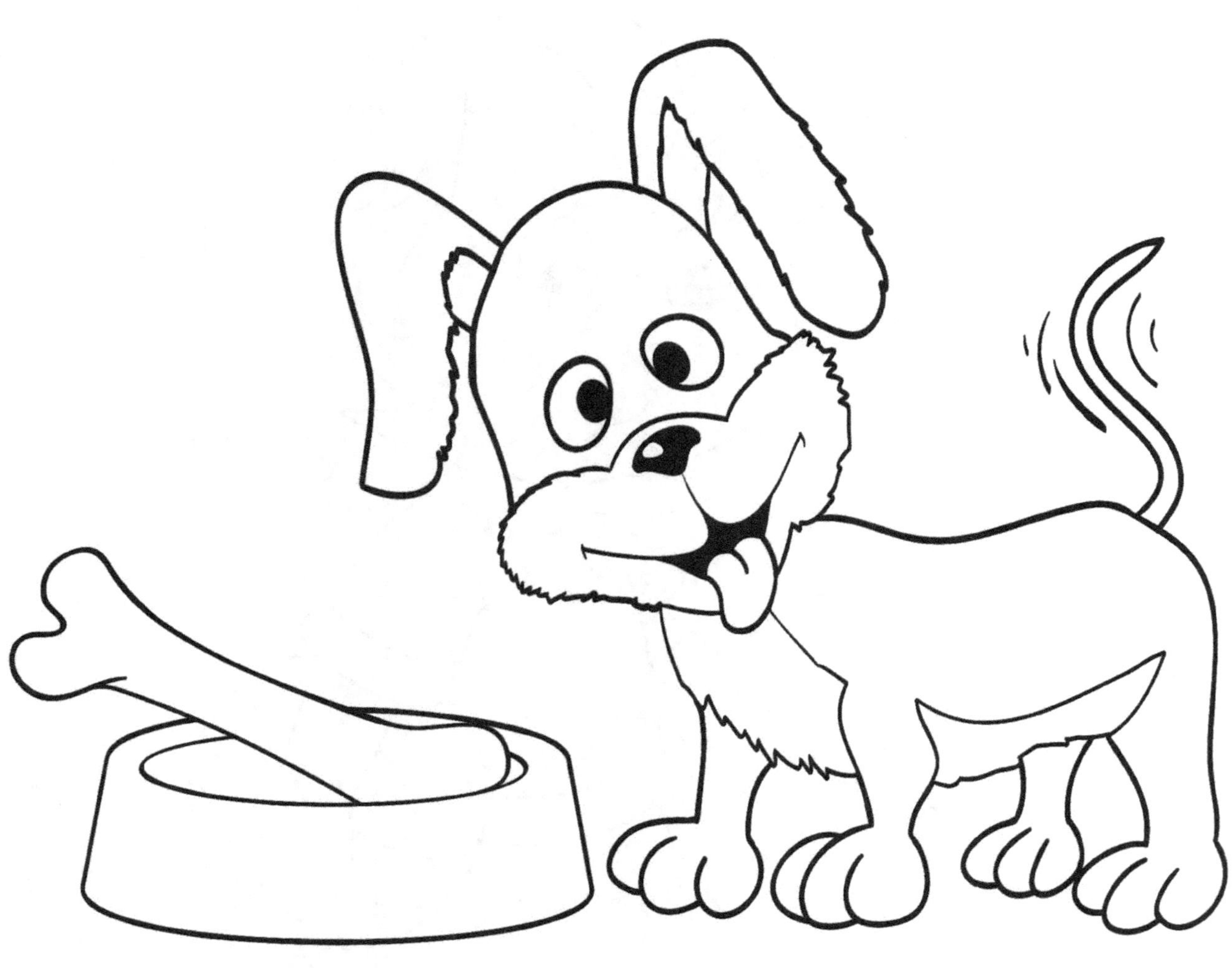

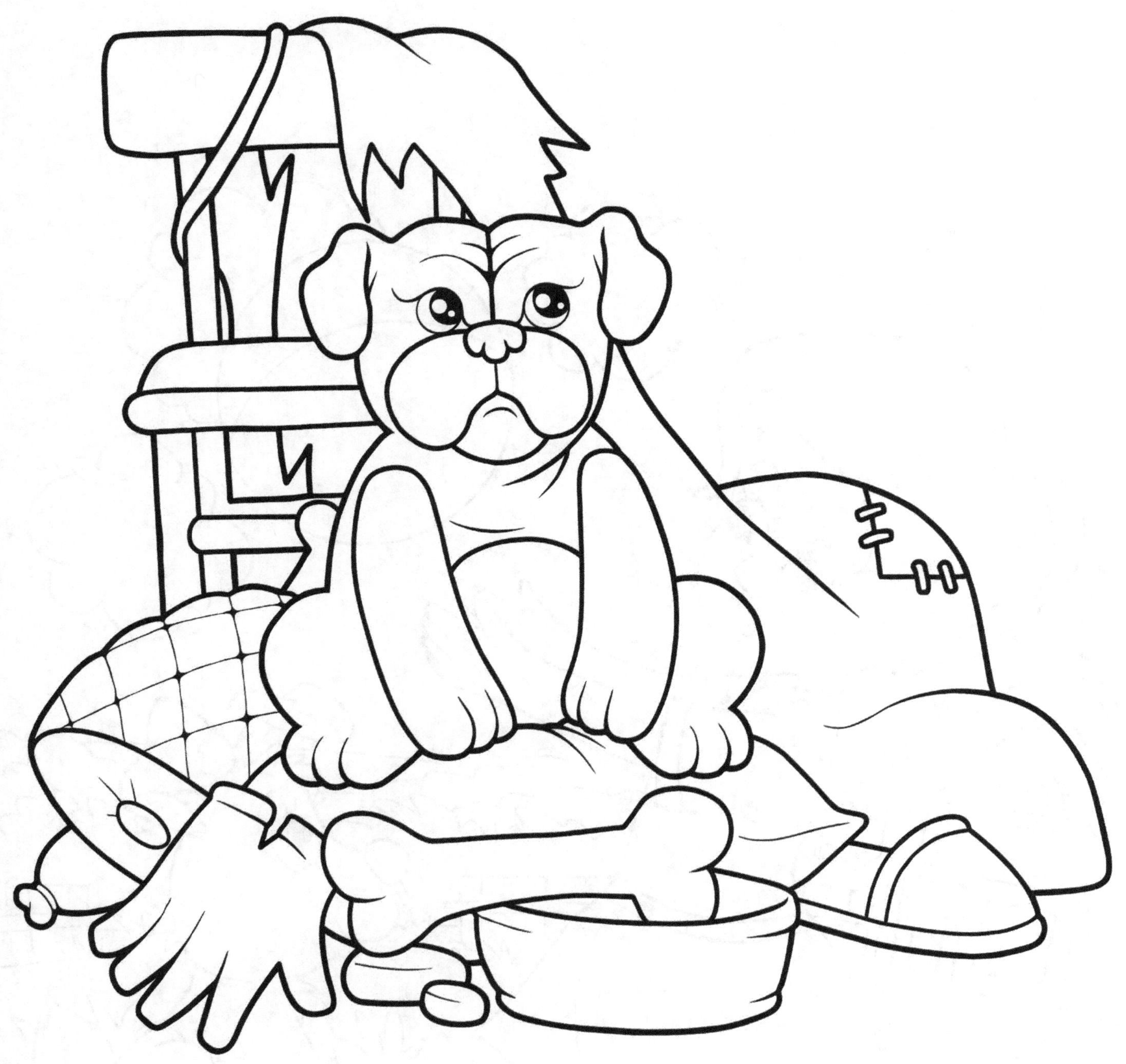

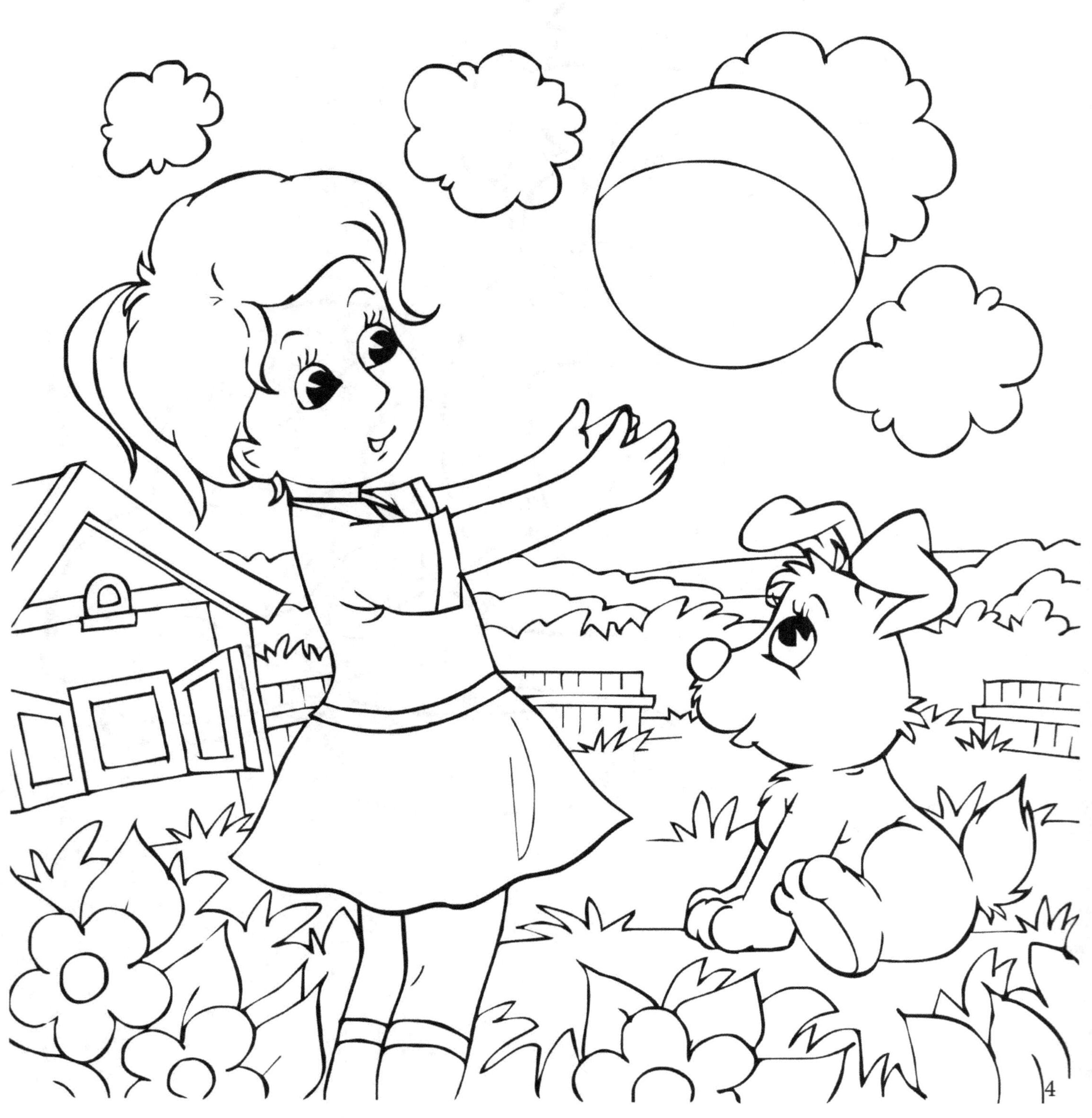

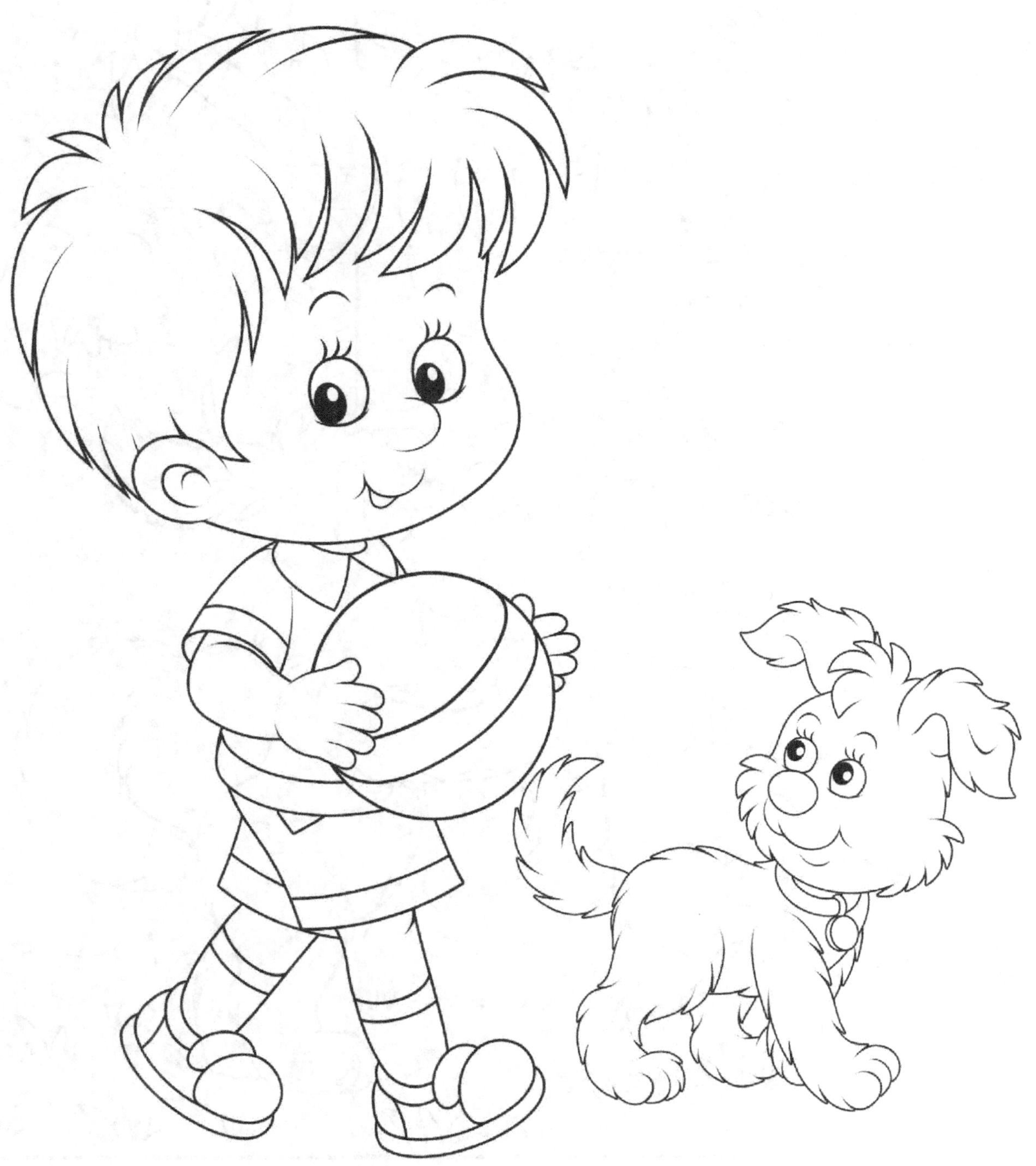

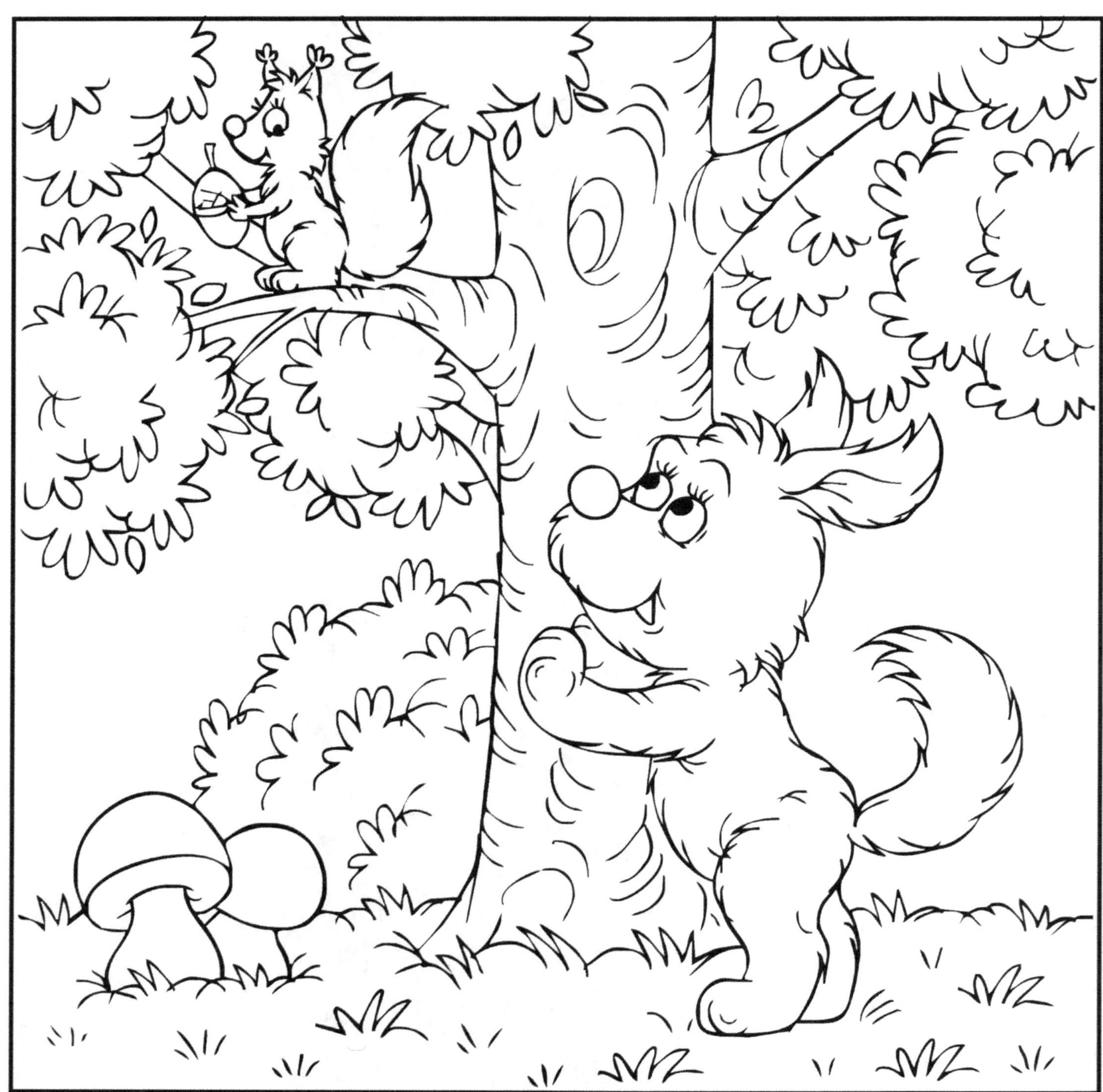

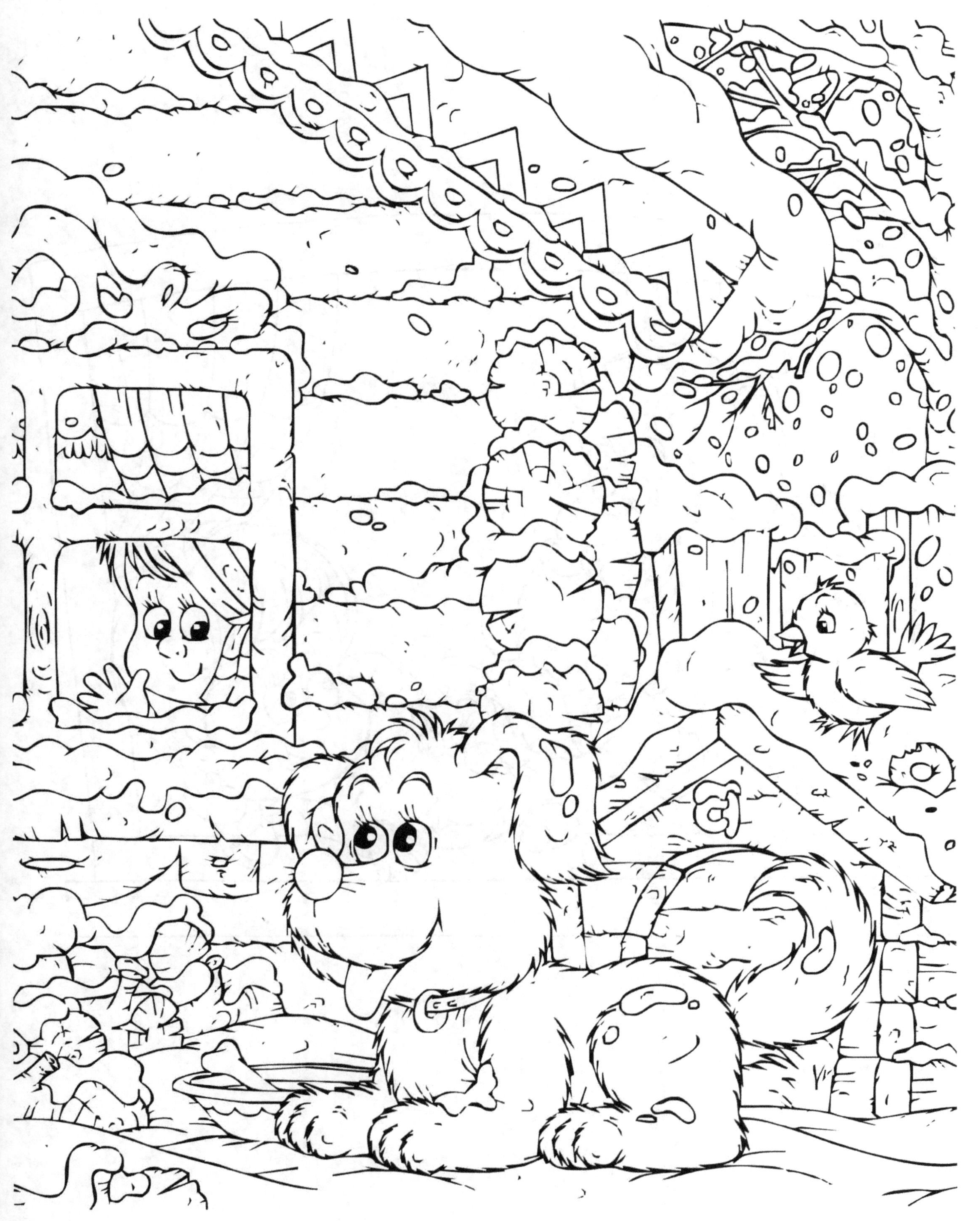

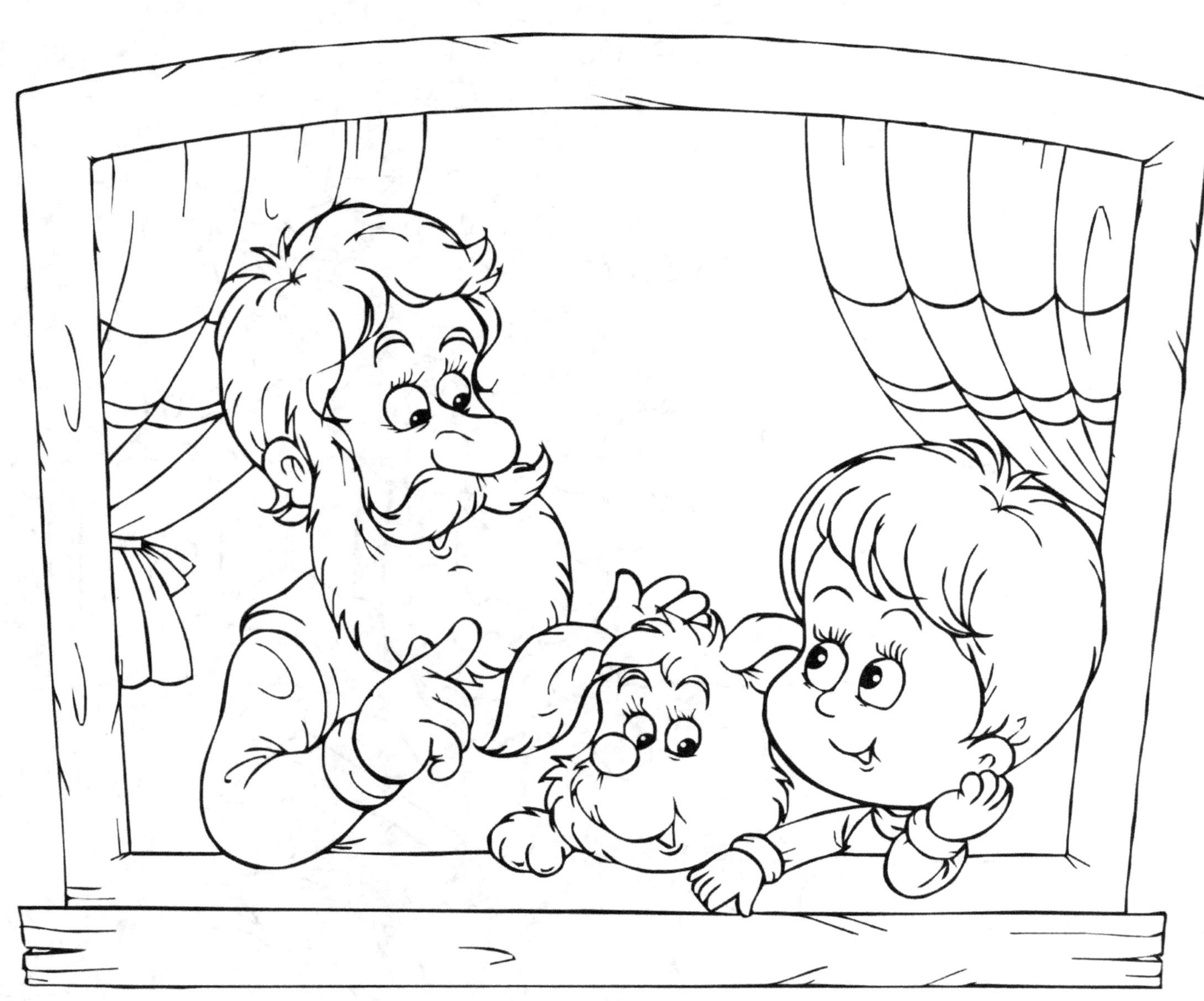

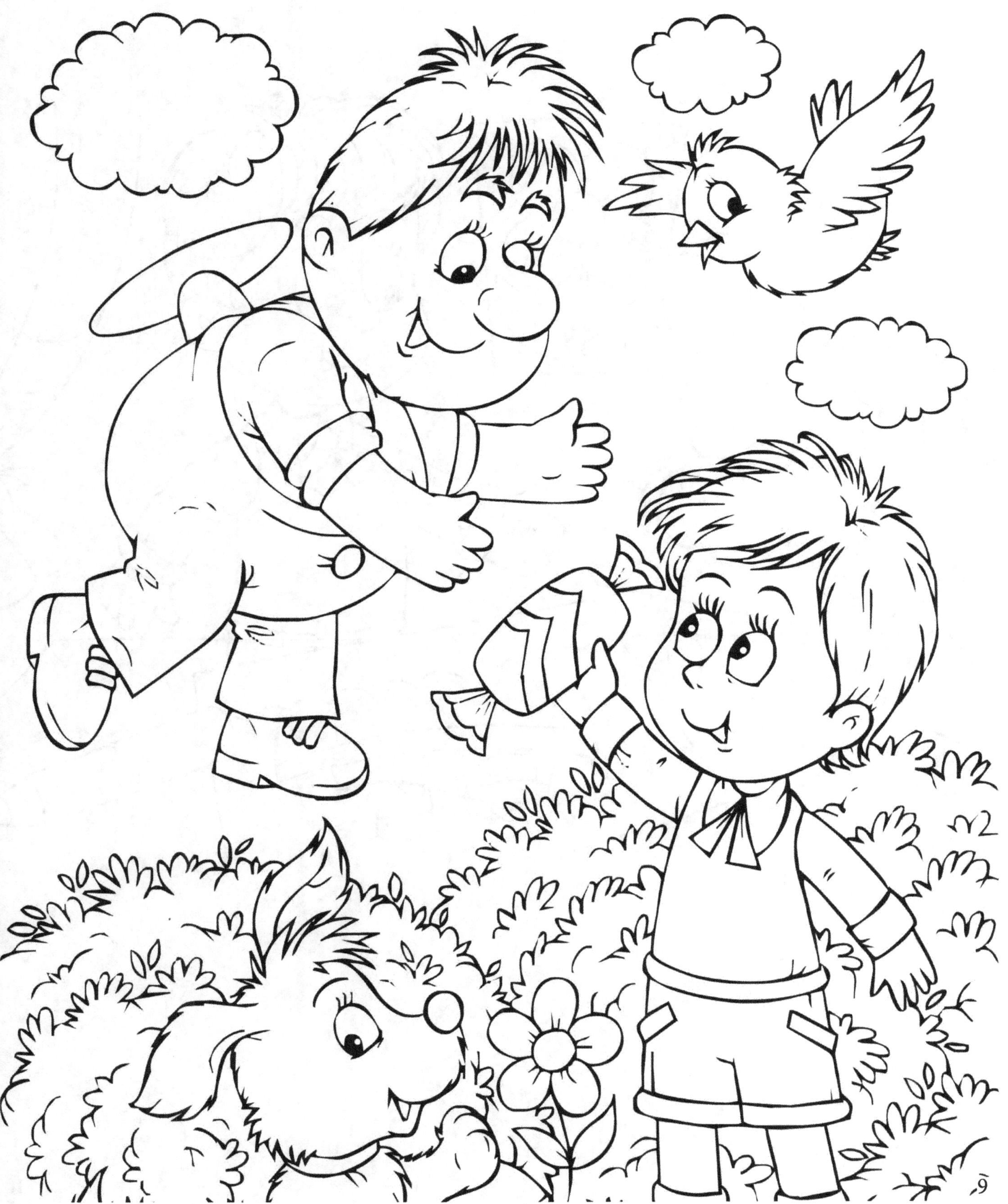

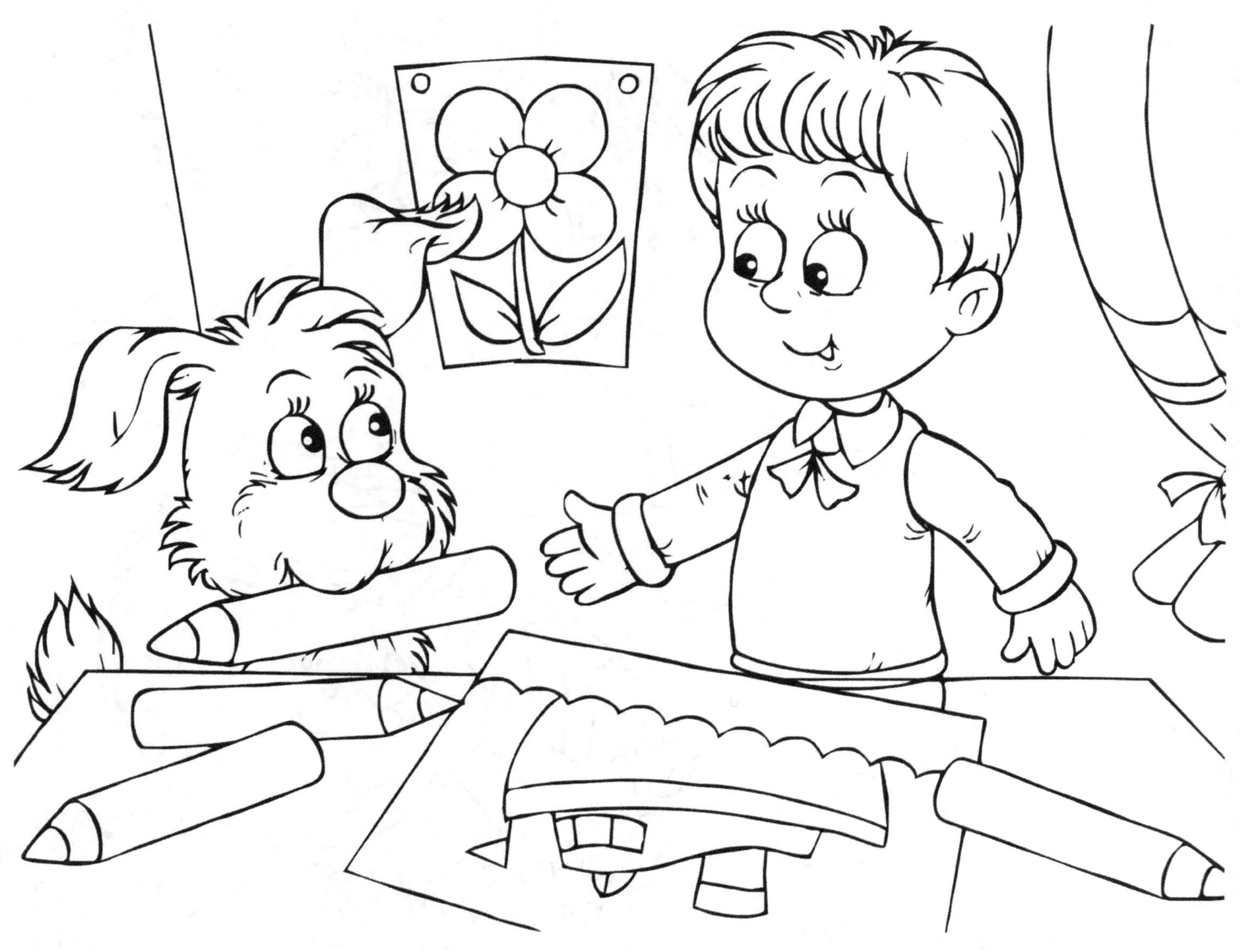

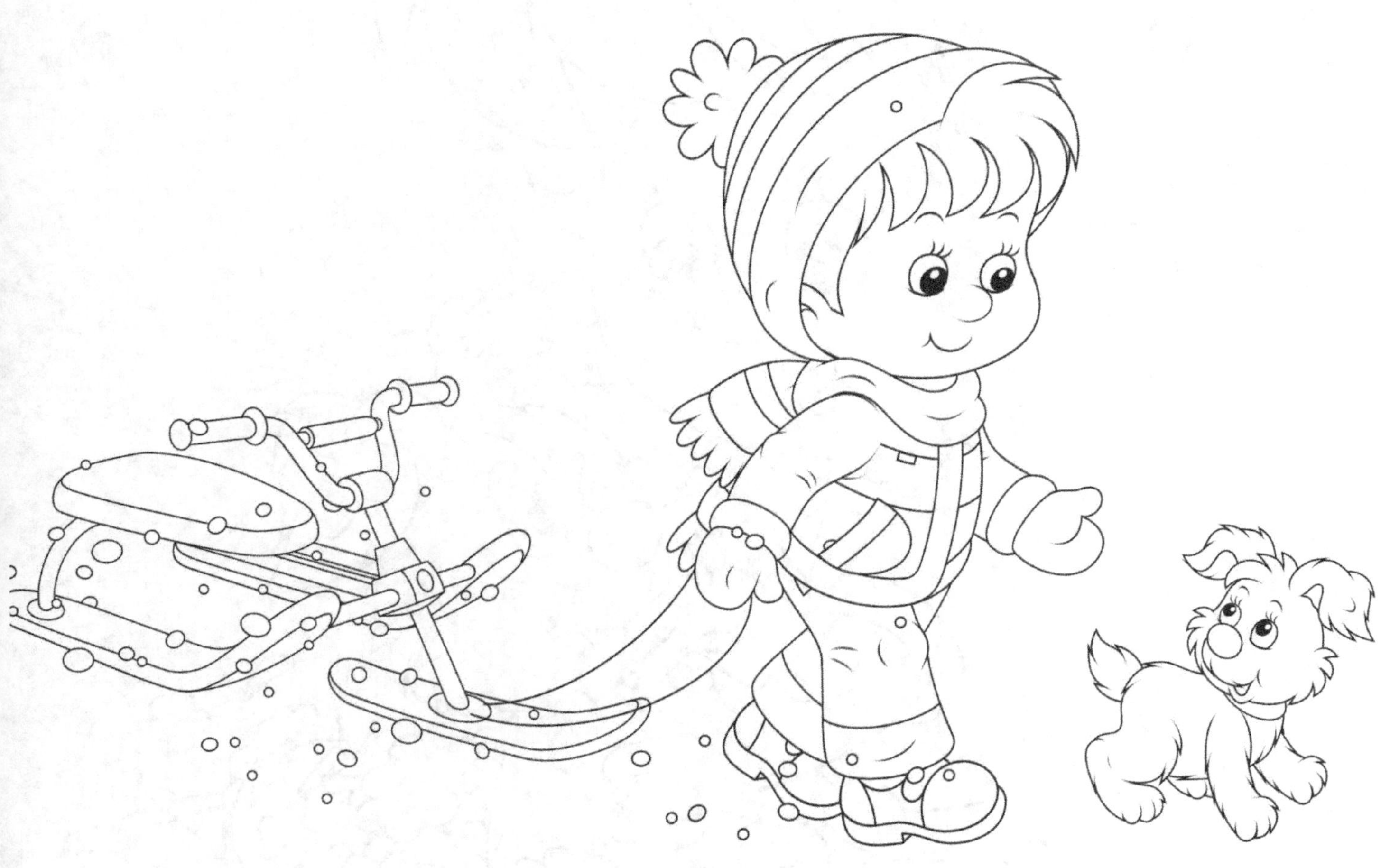

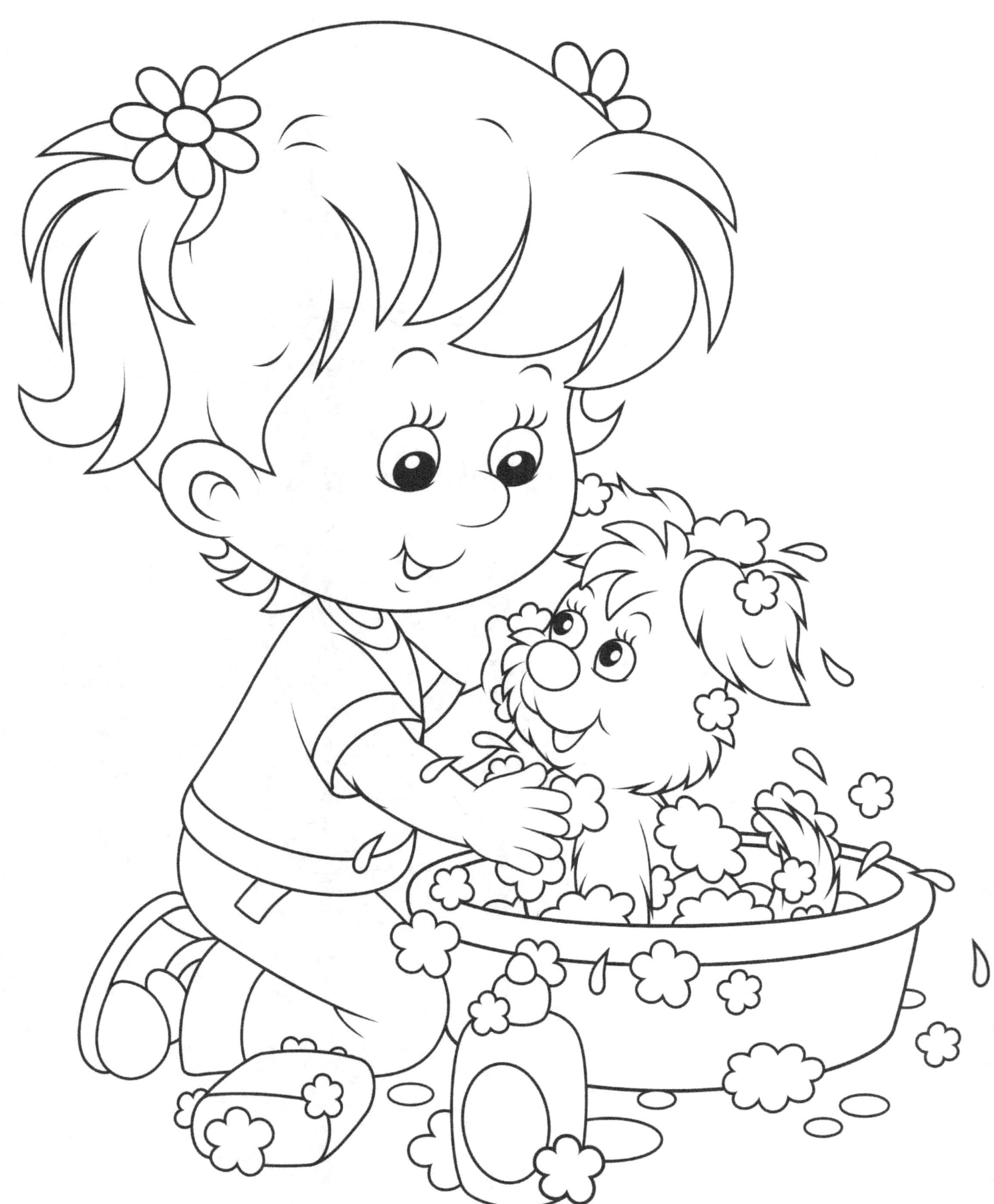

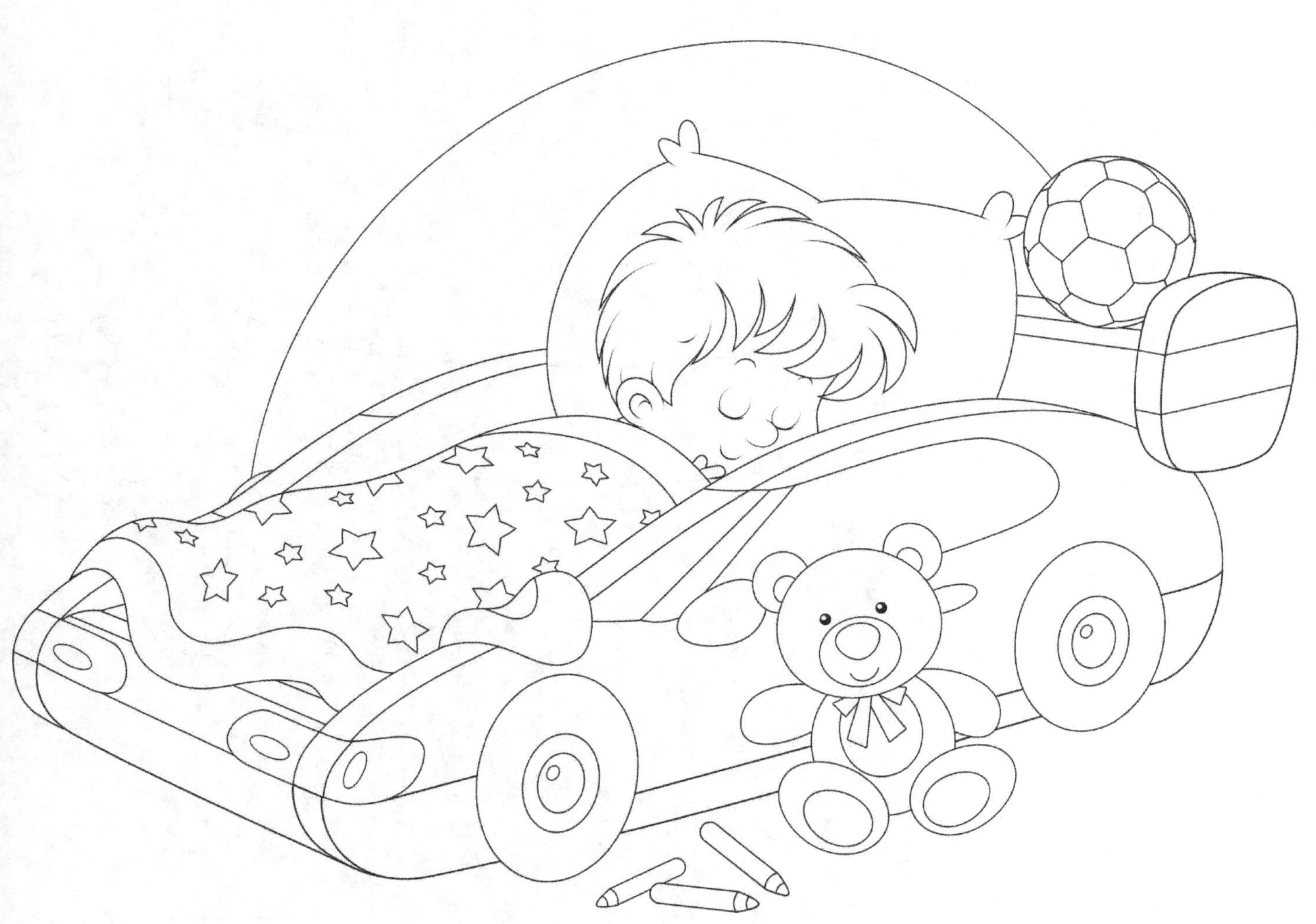

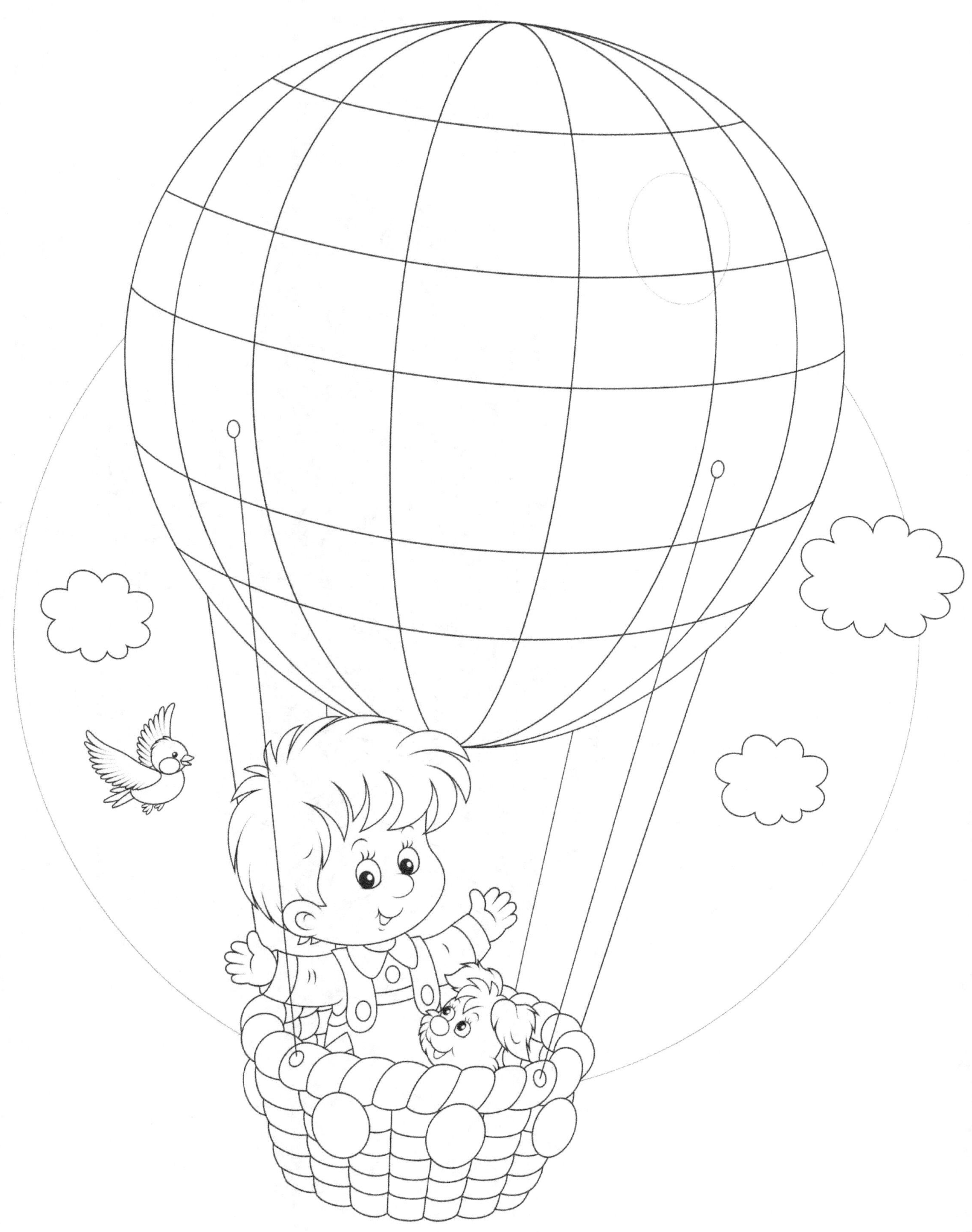

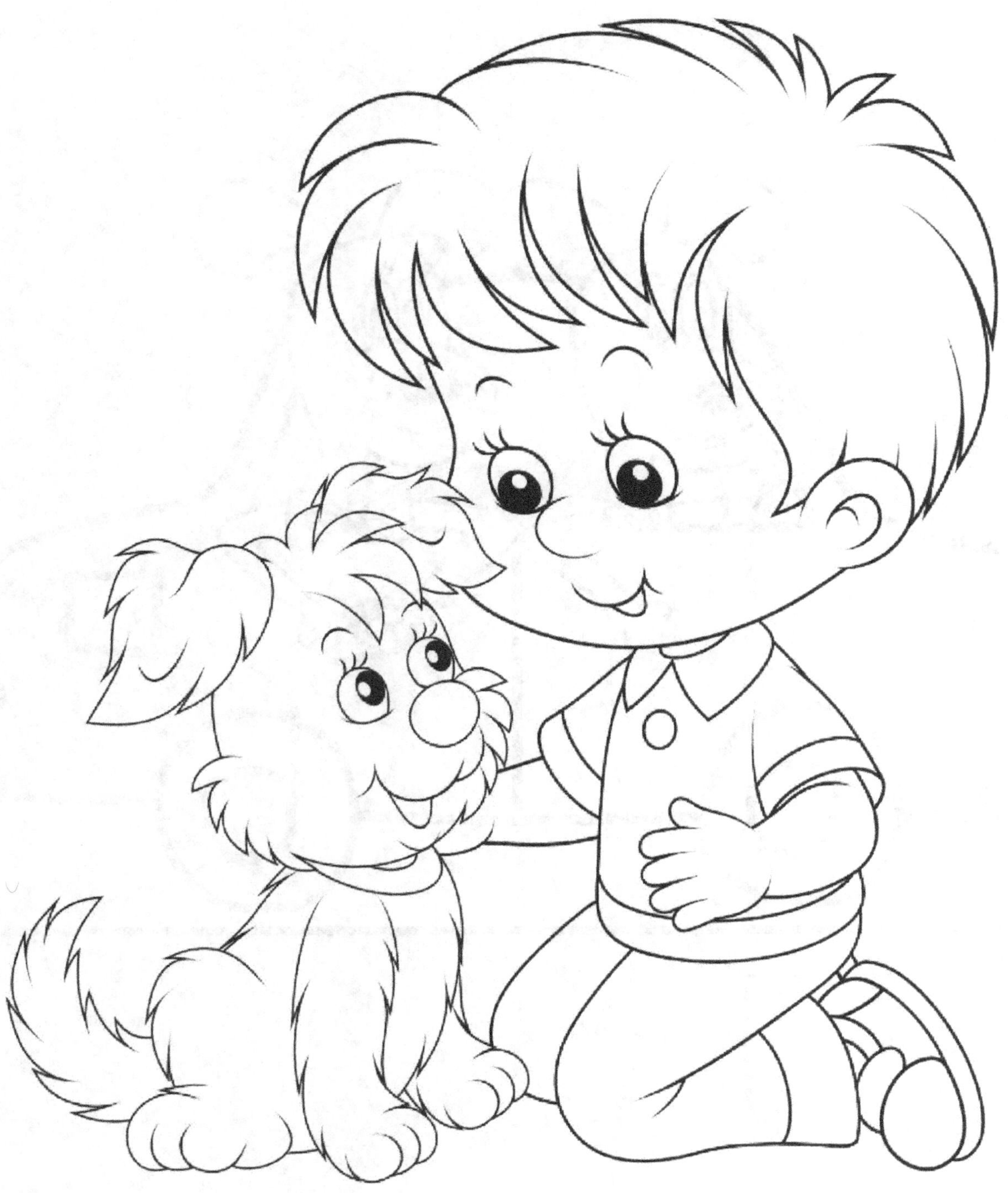

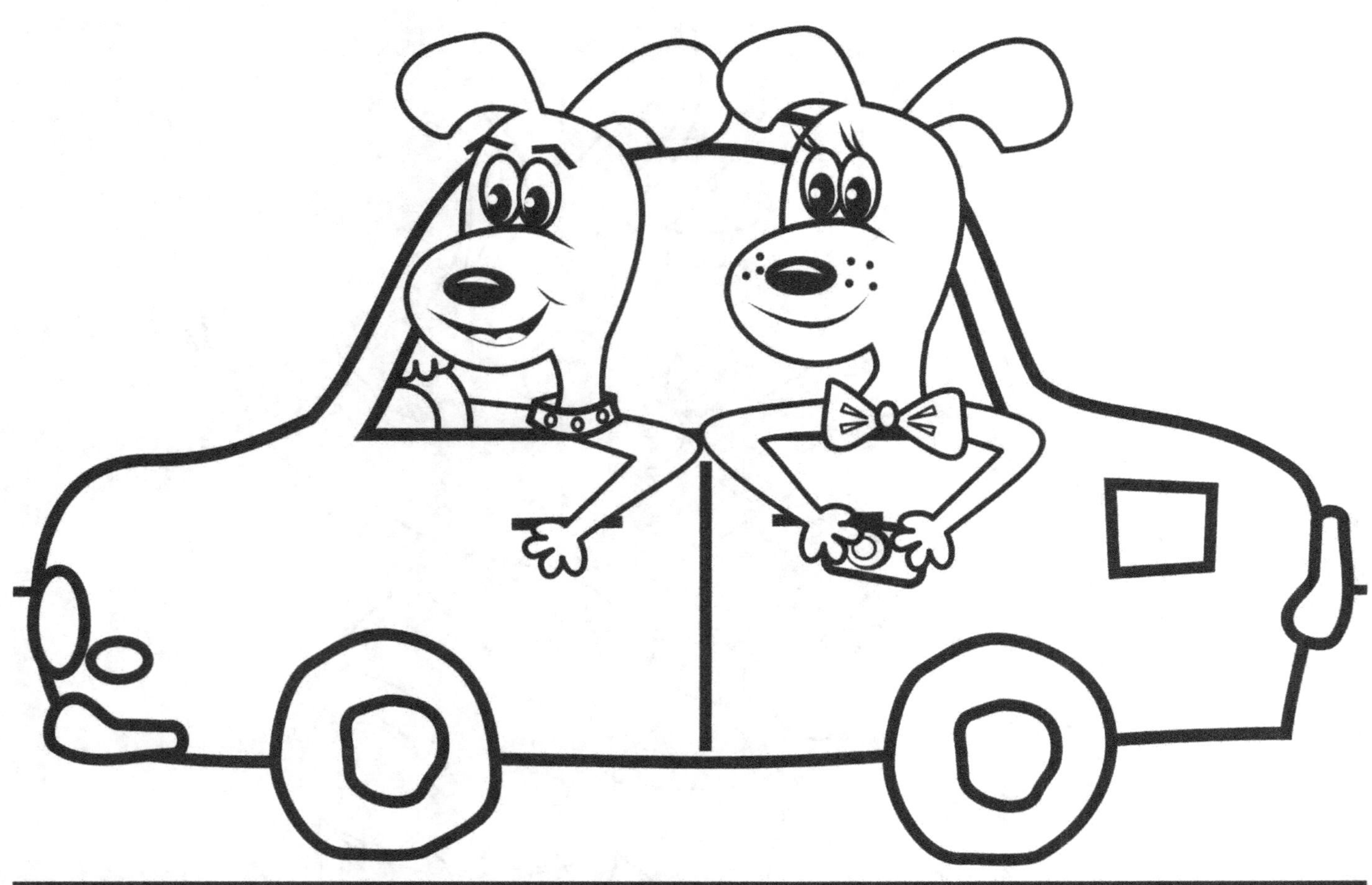

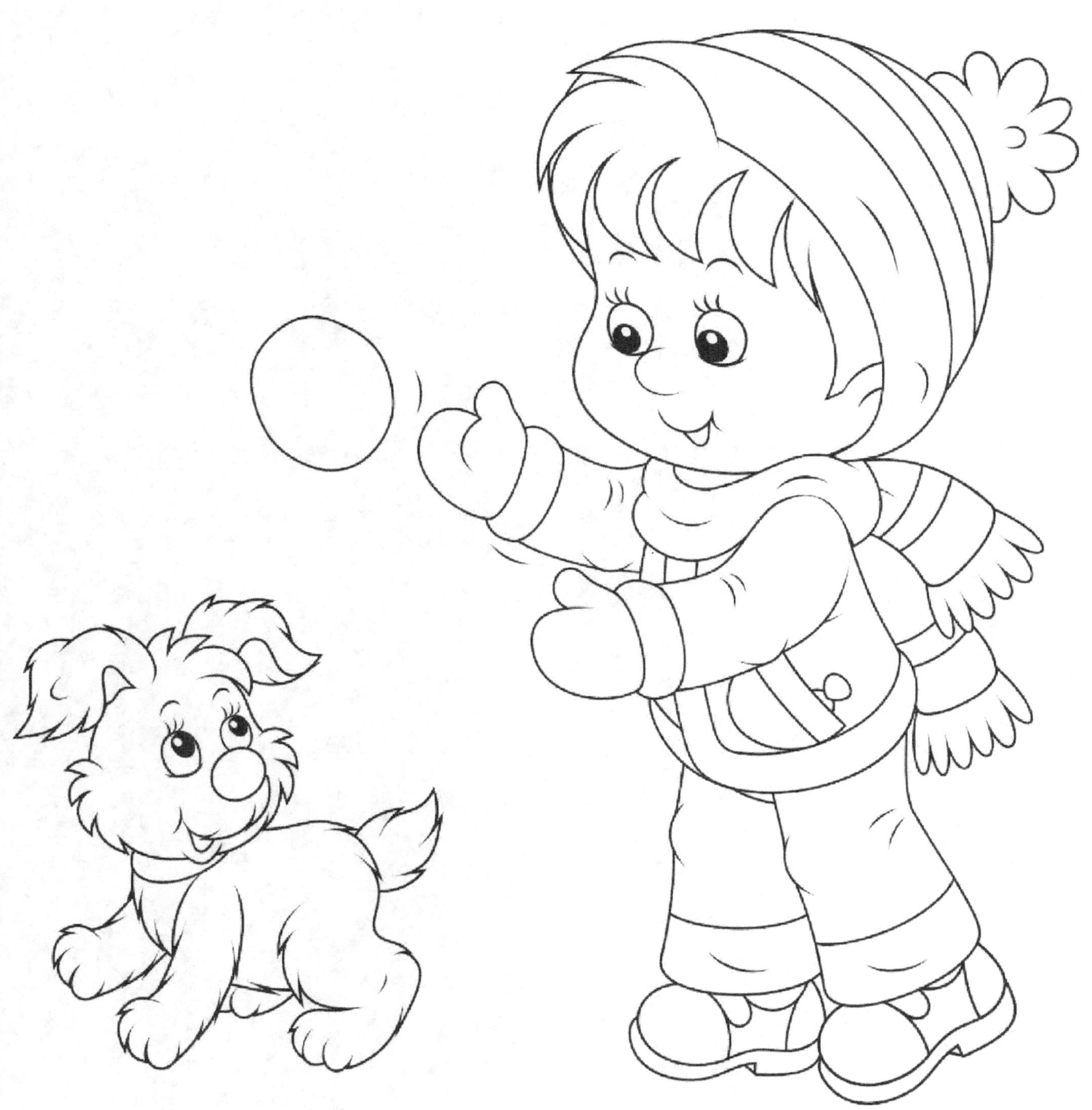

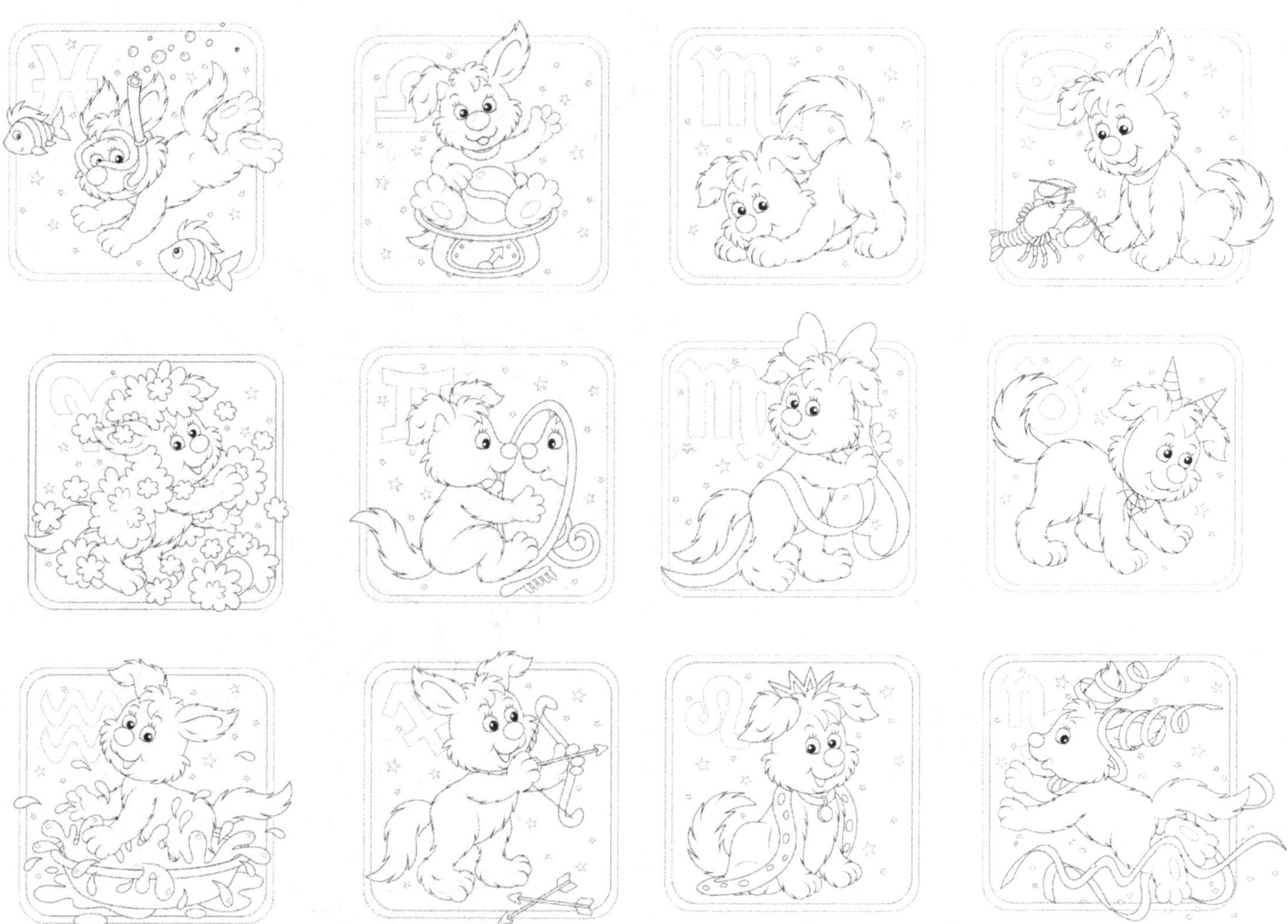

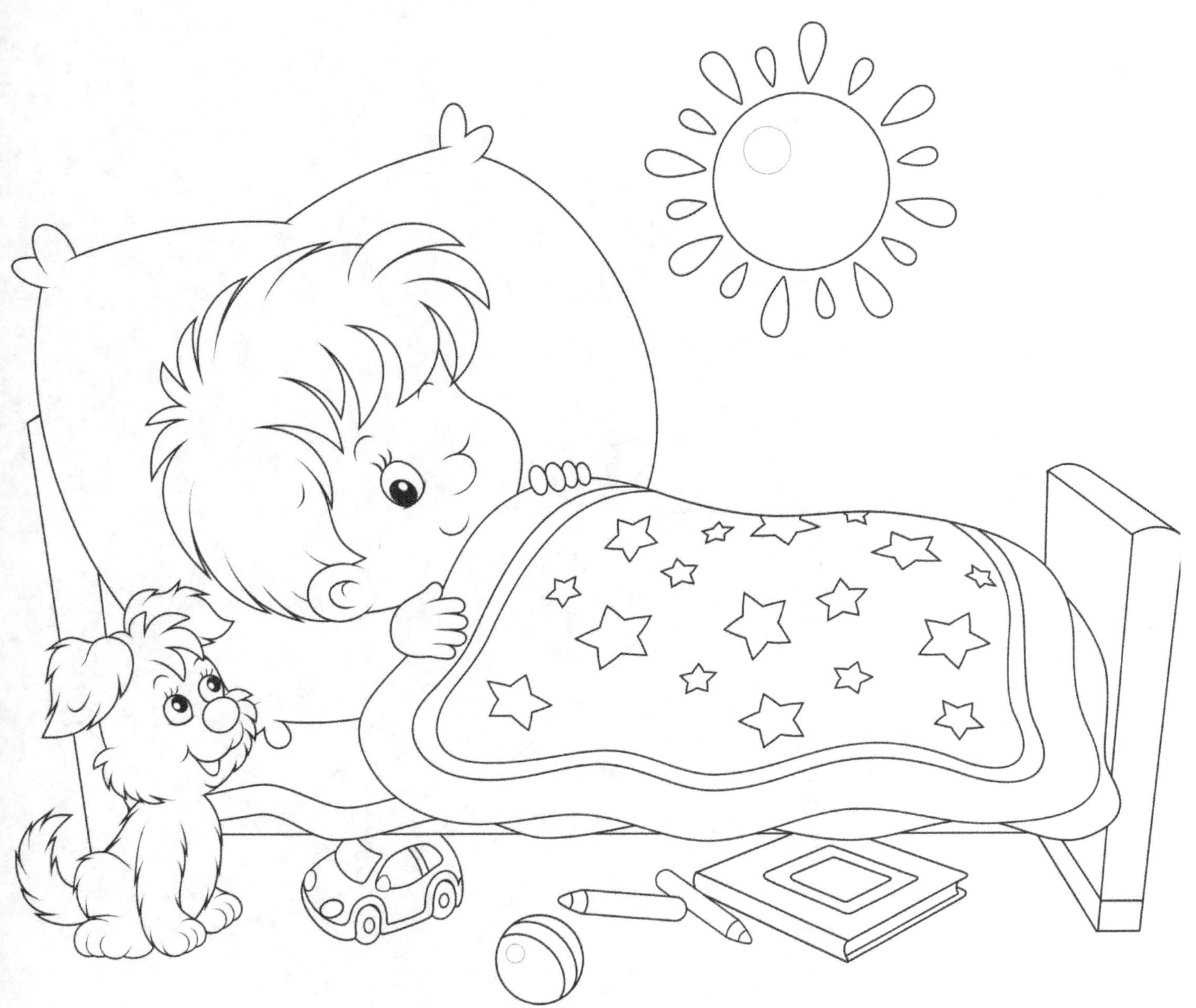

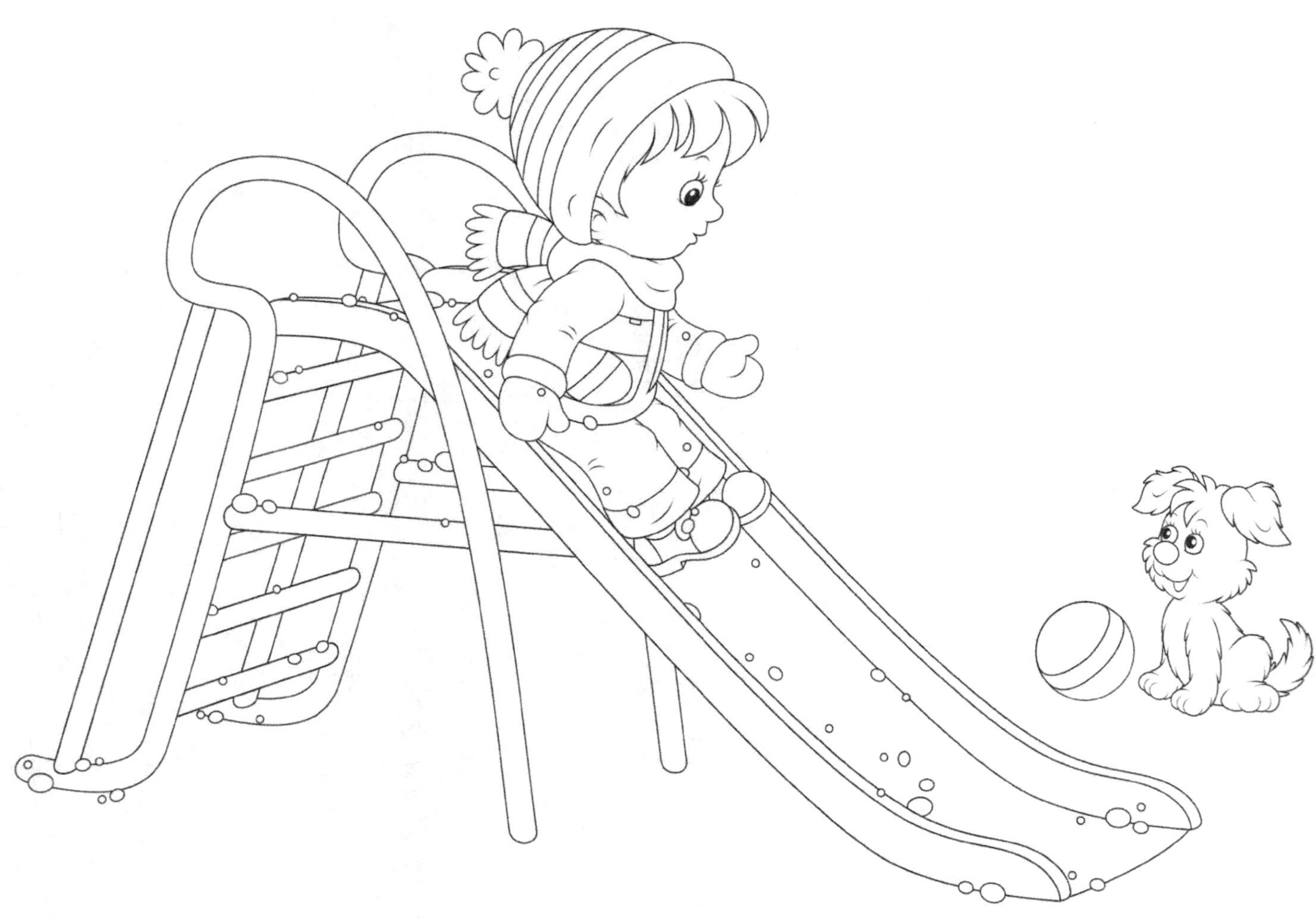

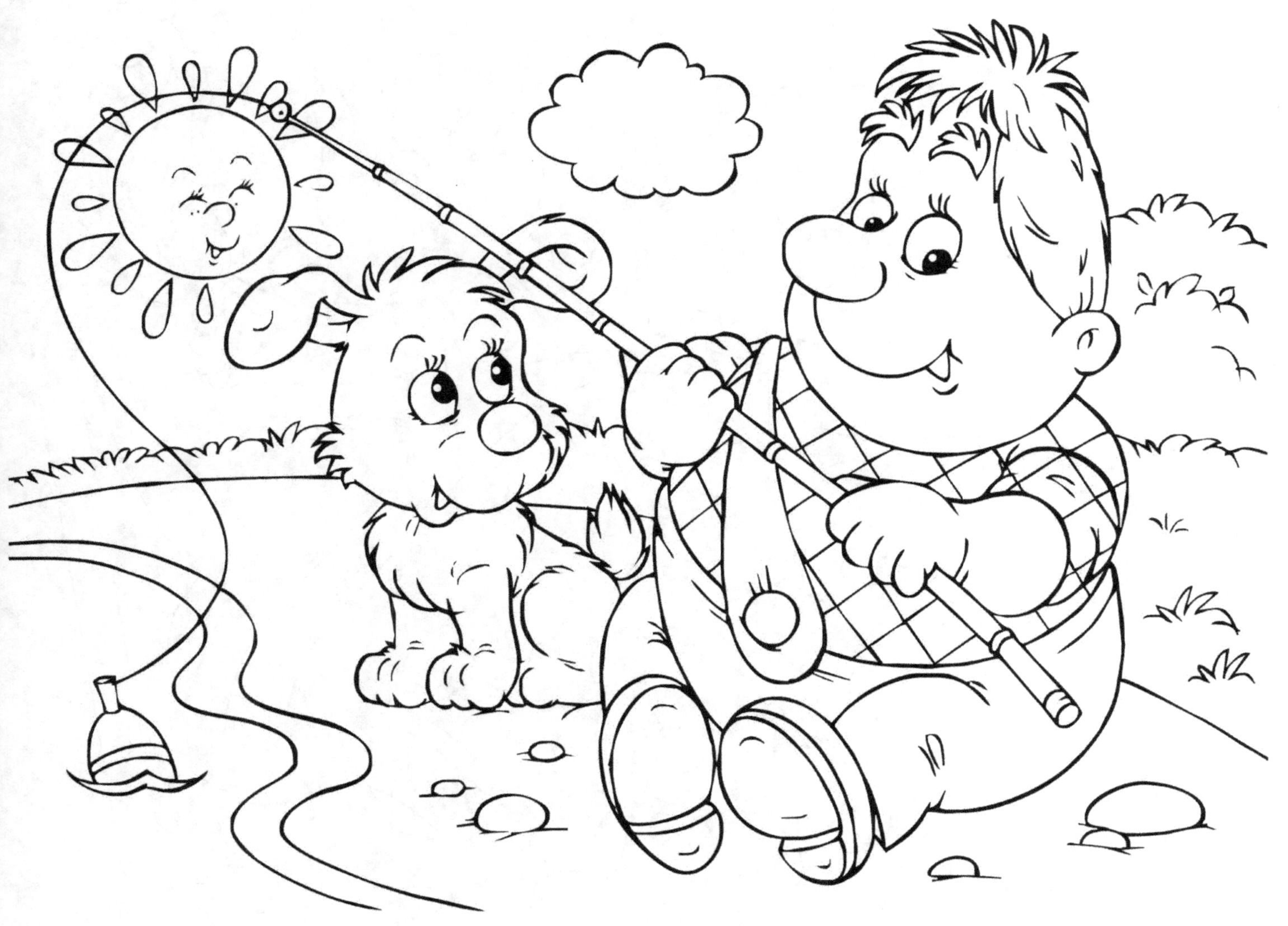

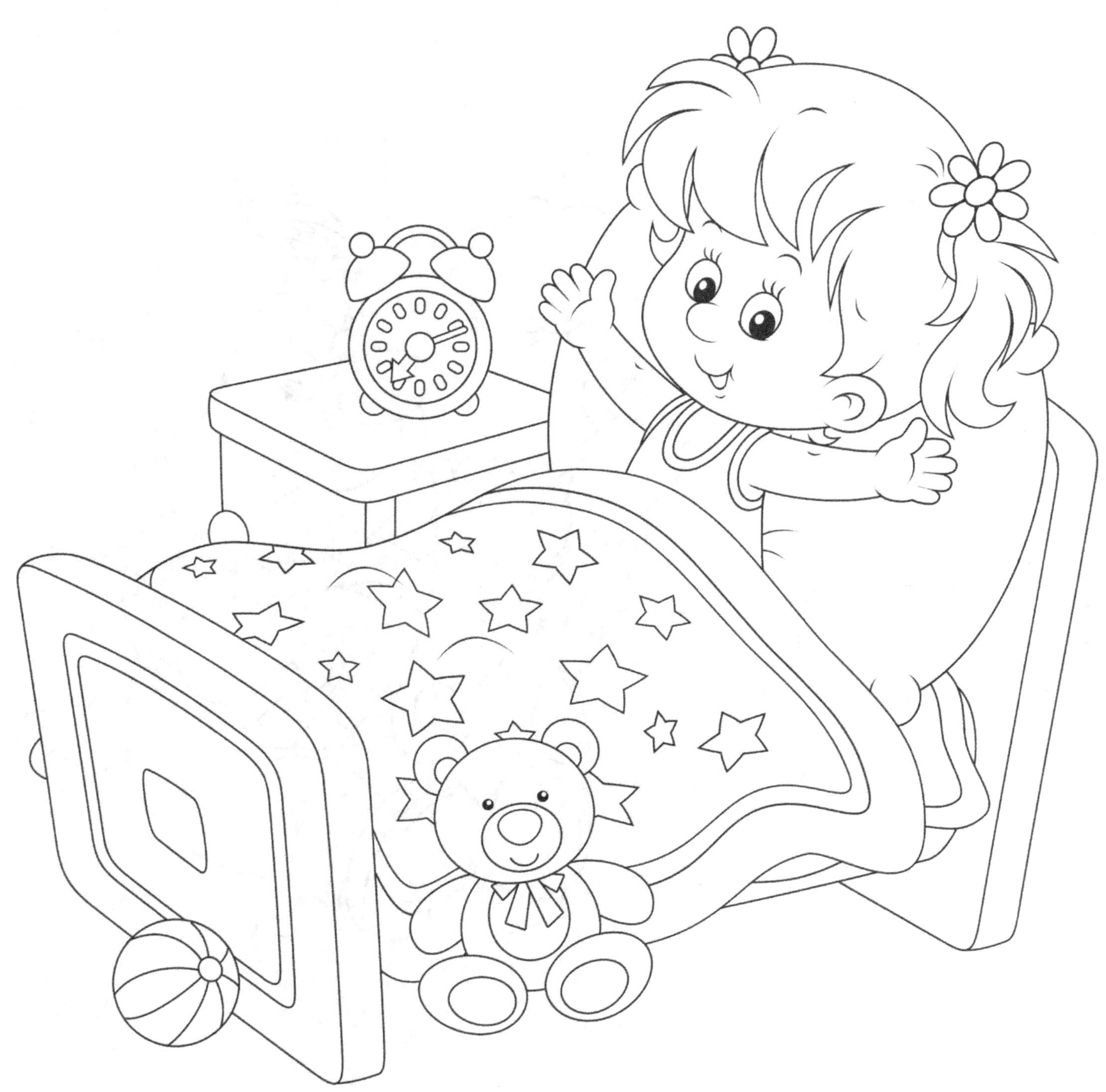

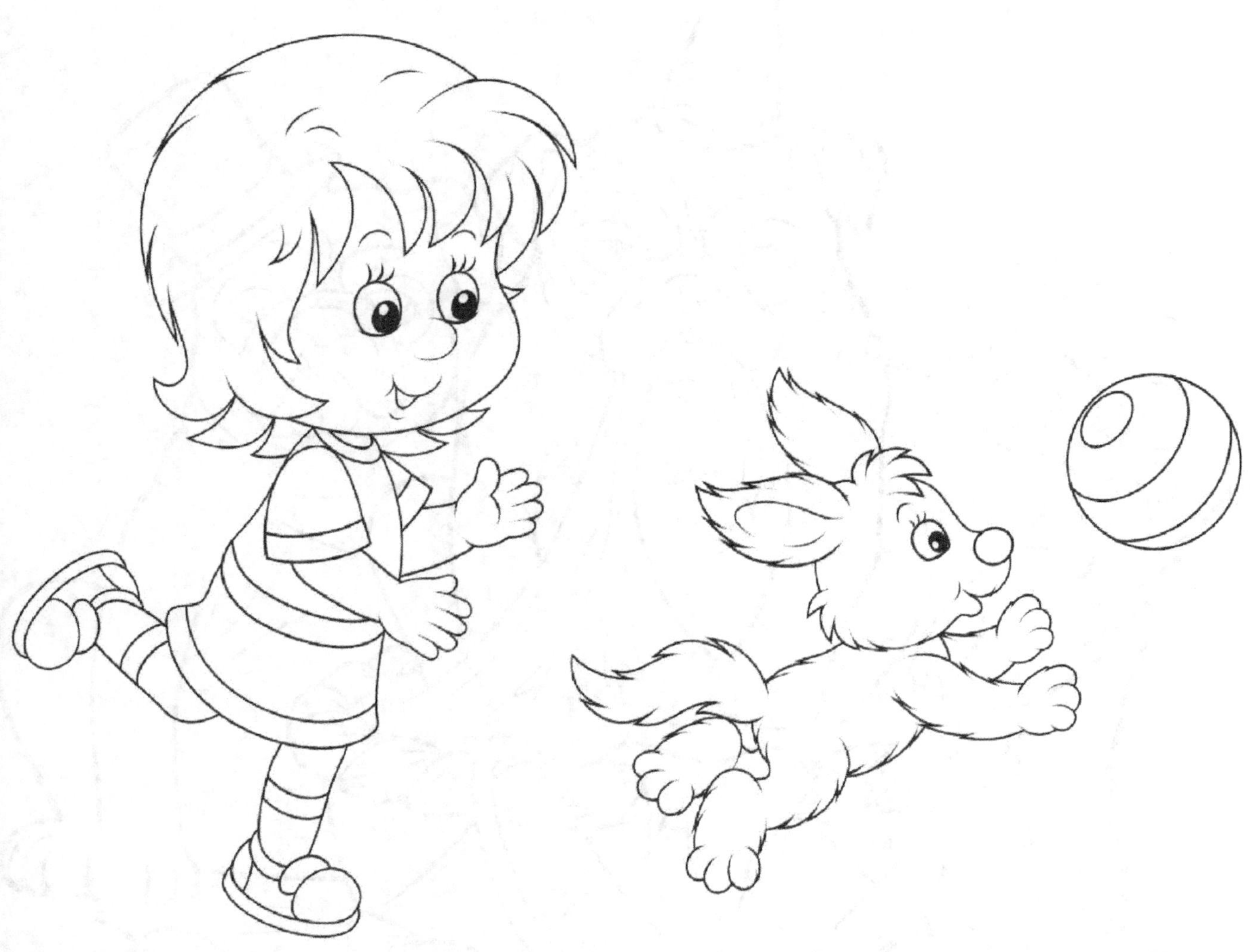

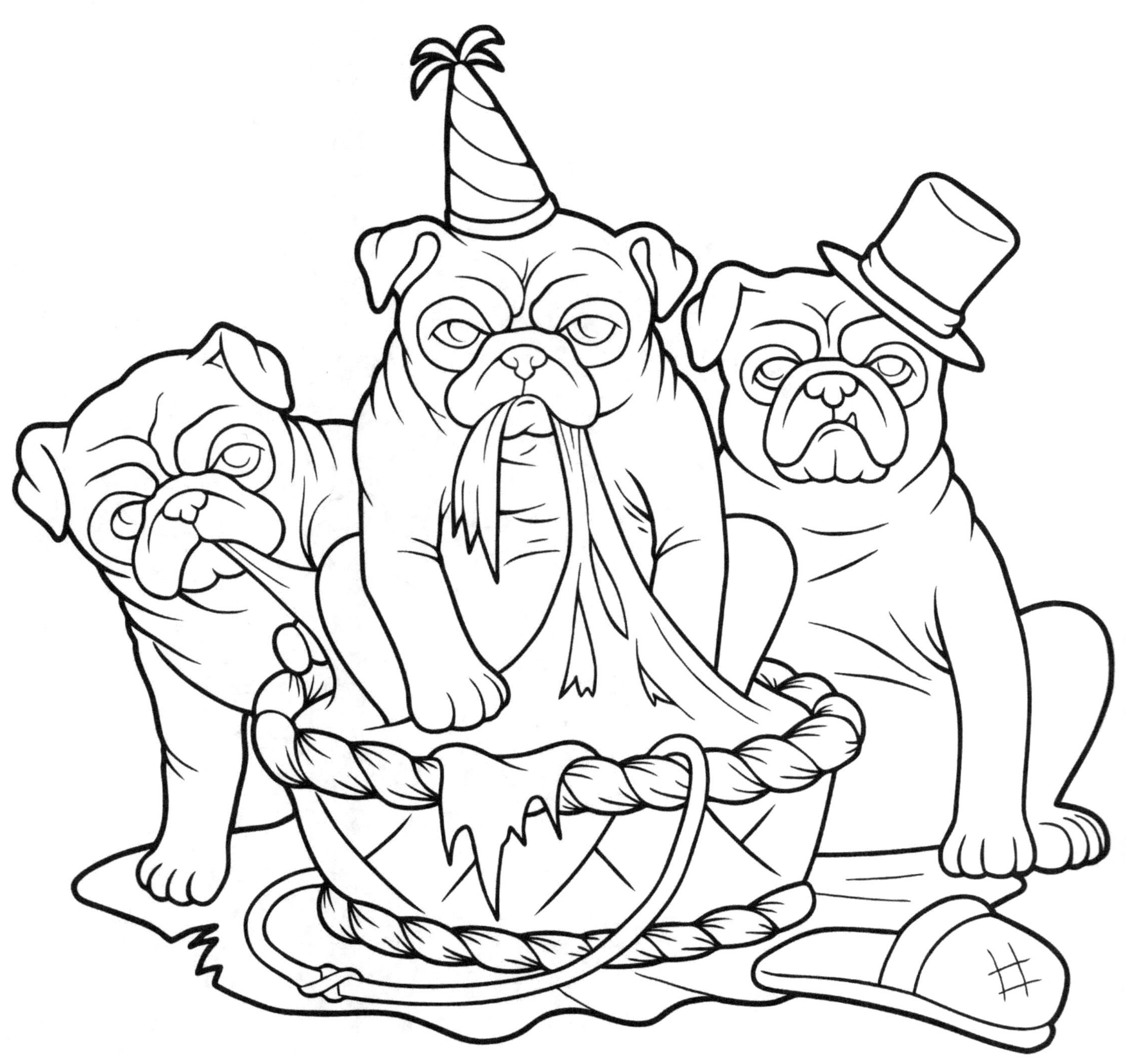

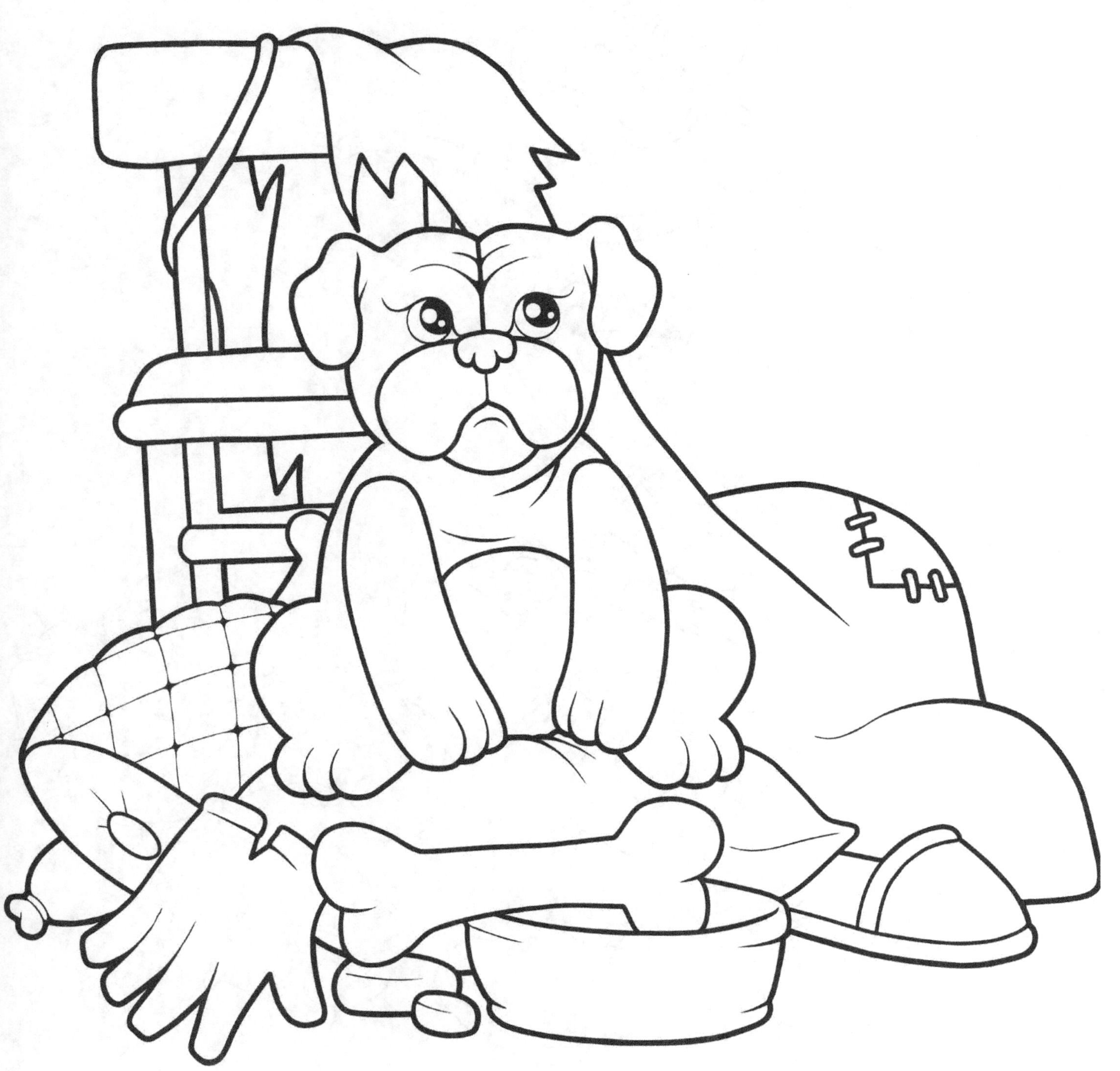

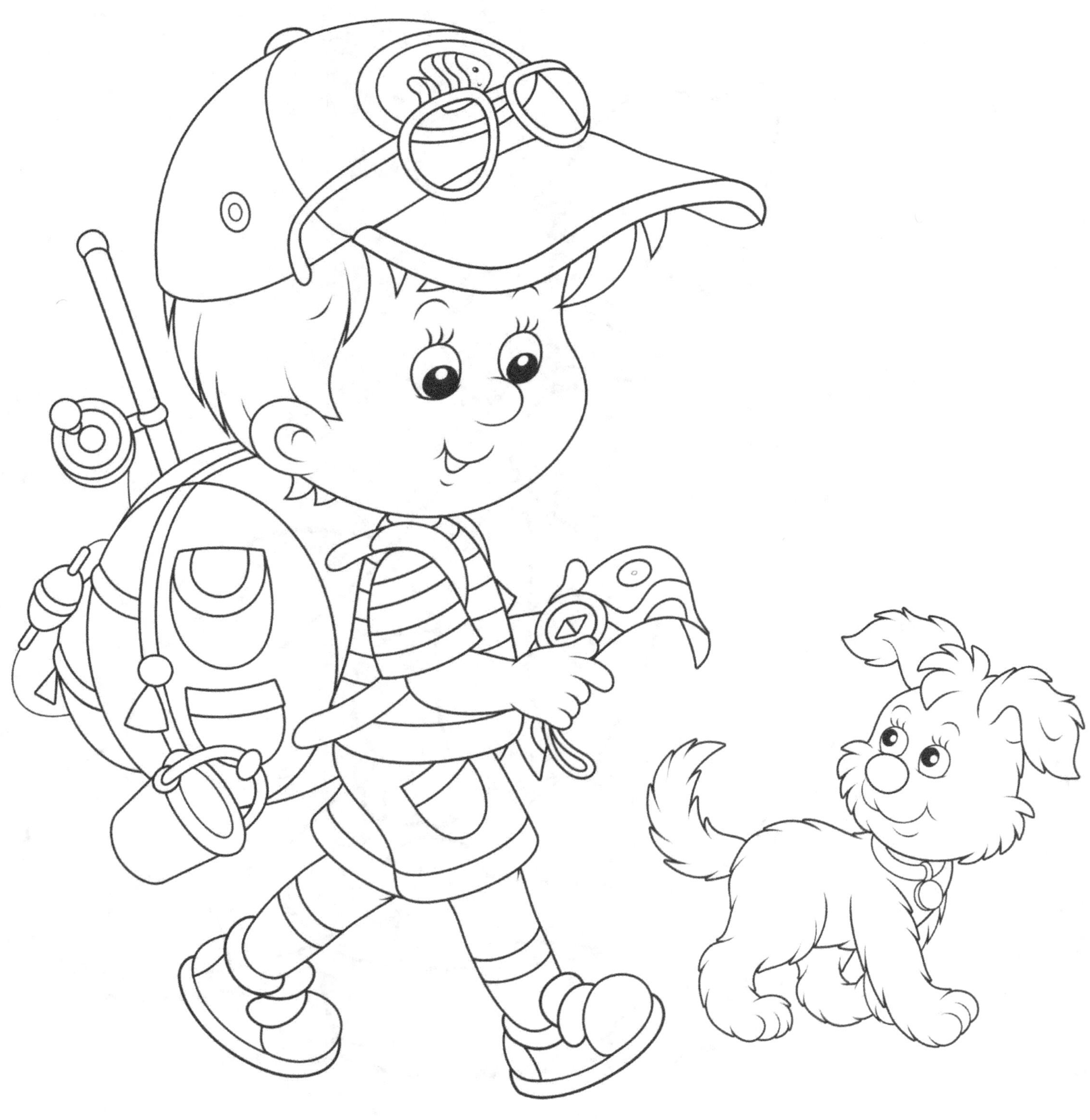

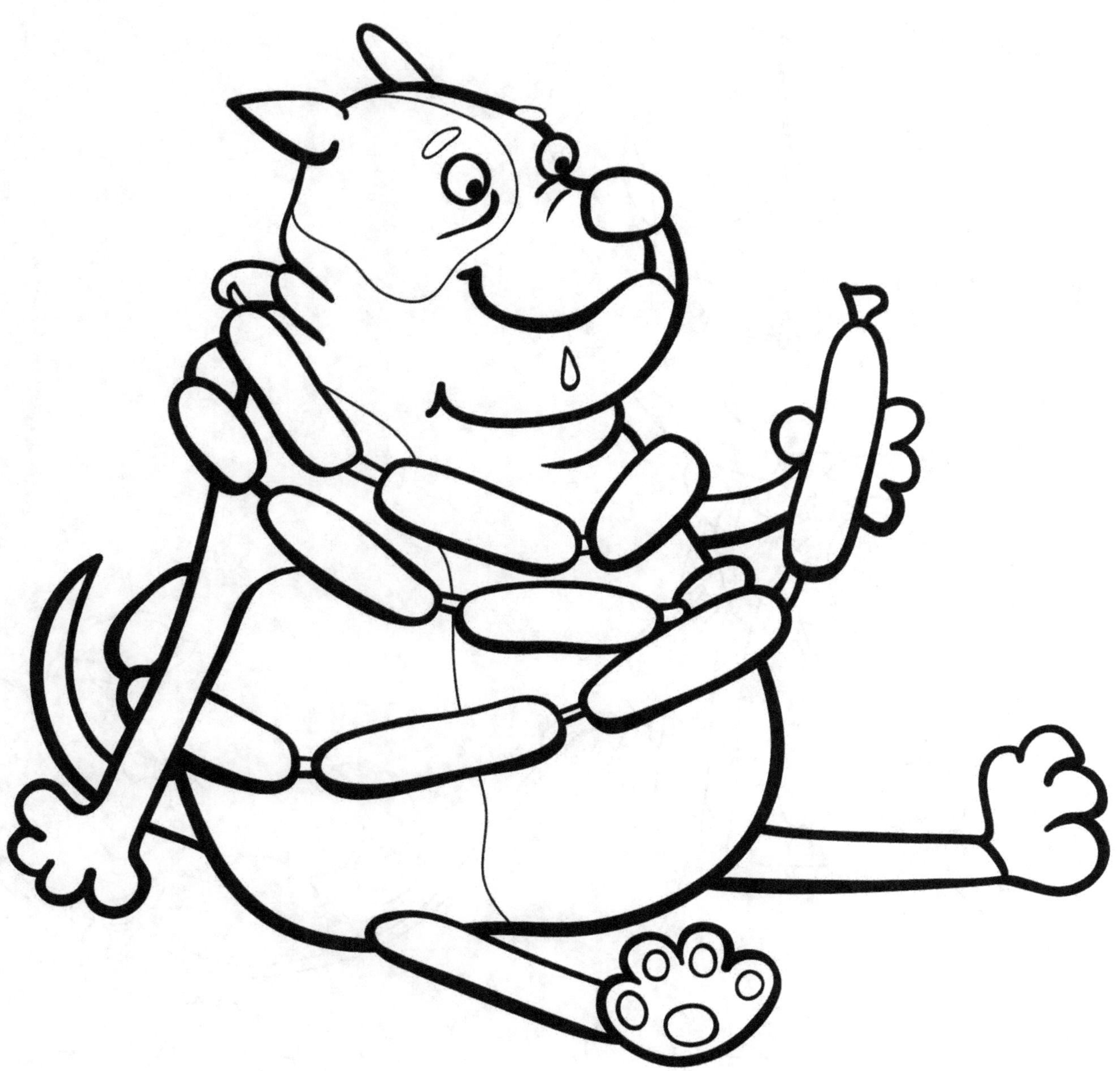

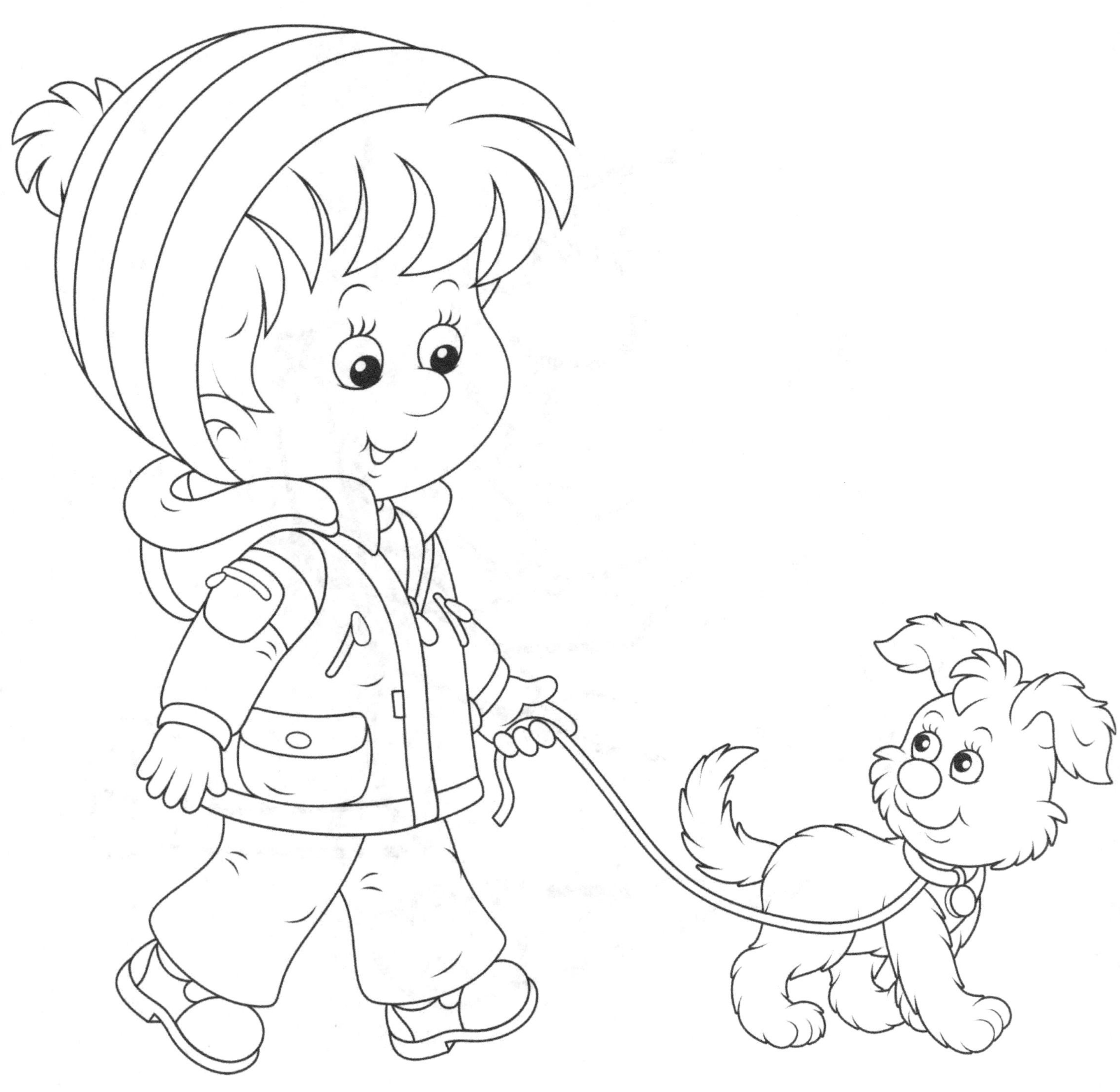

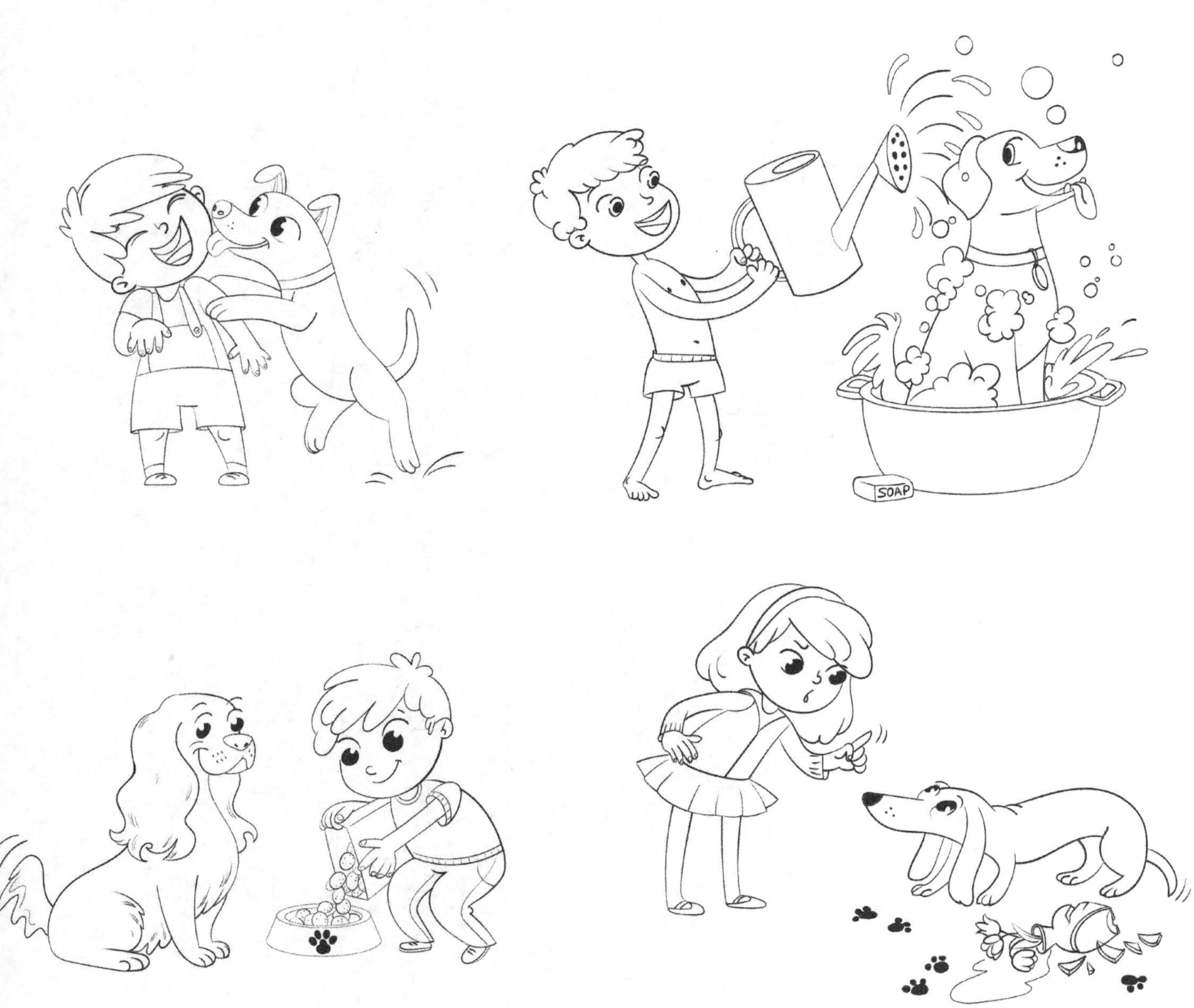
SOAP

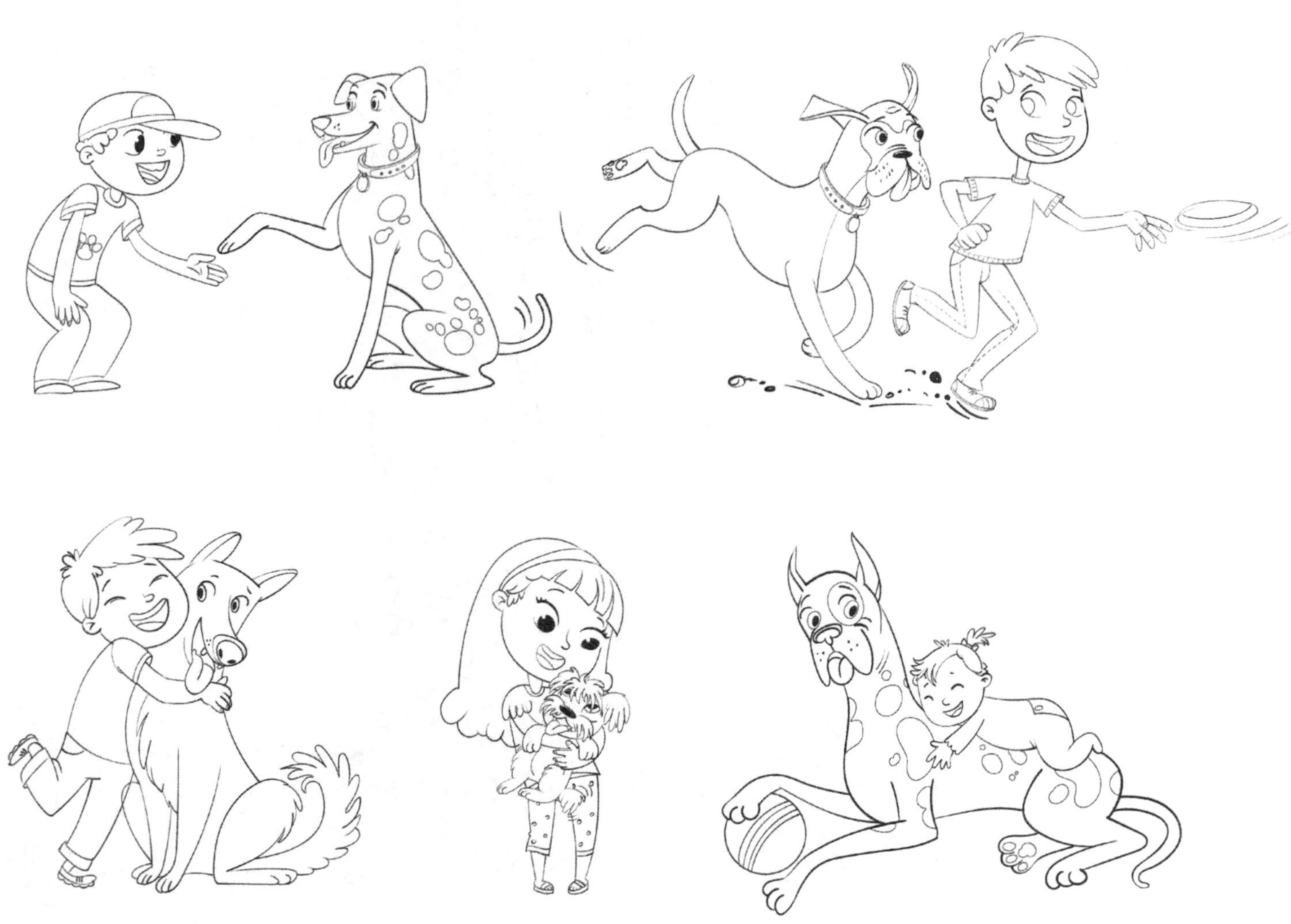

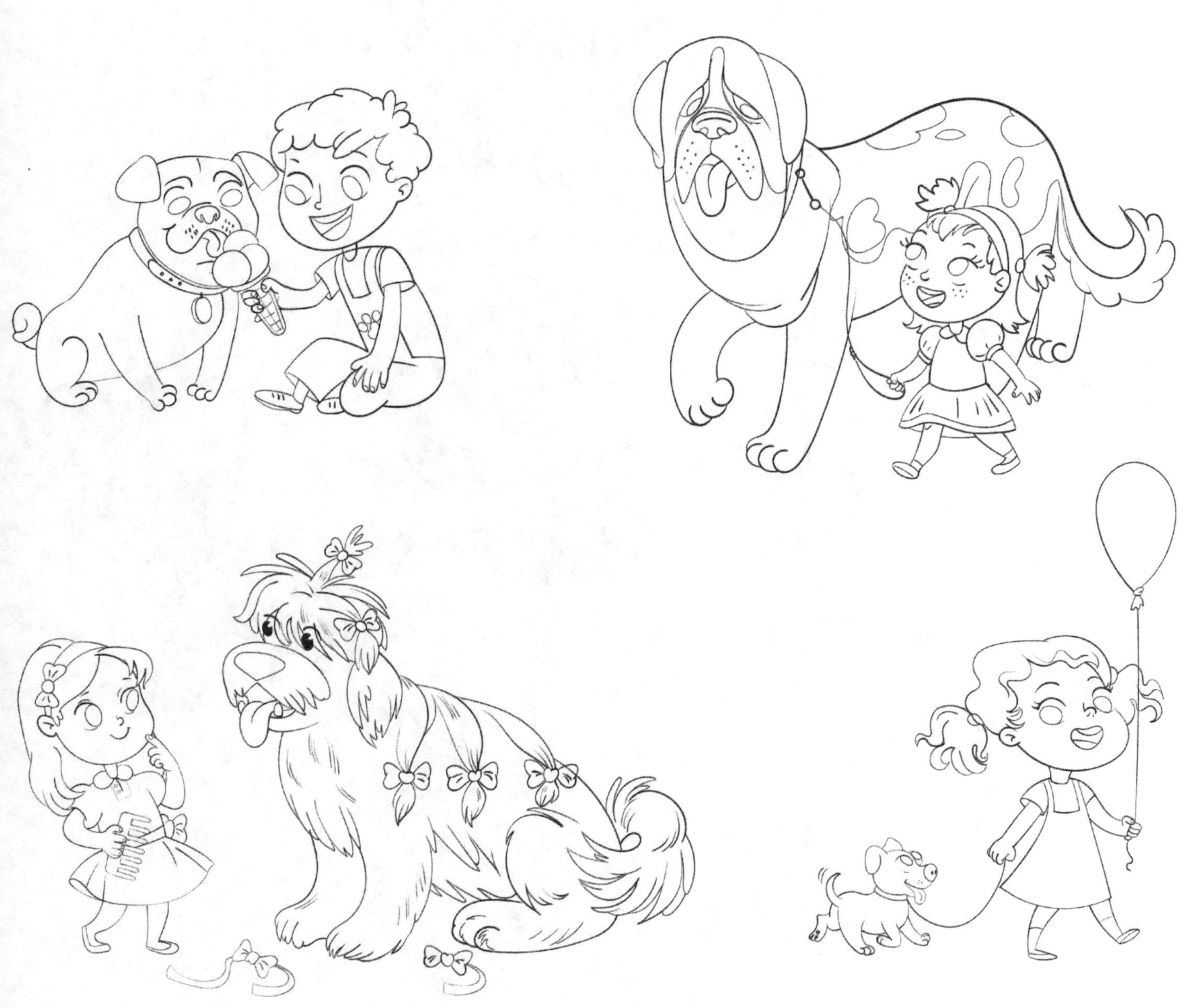

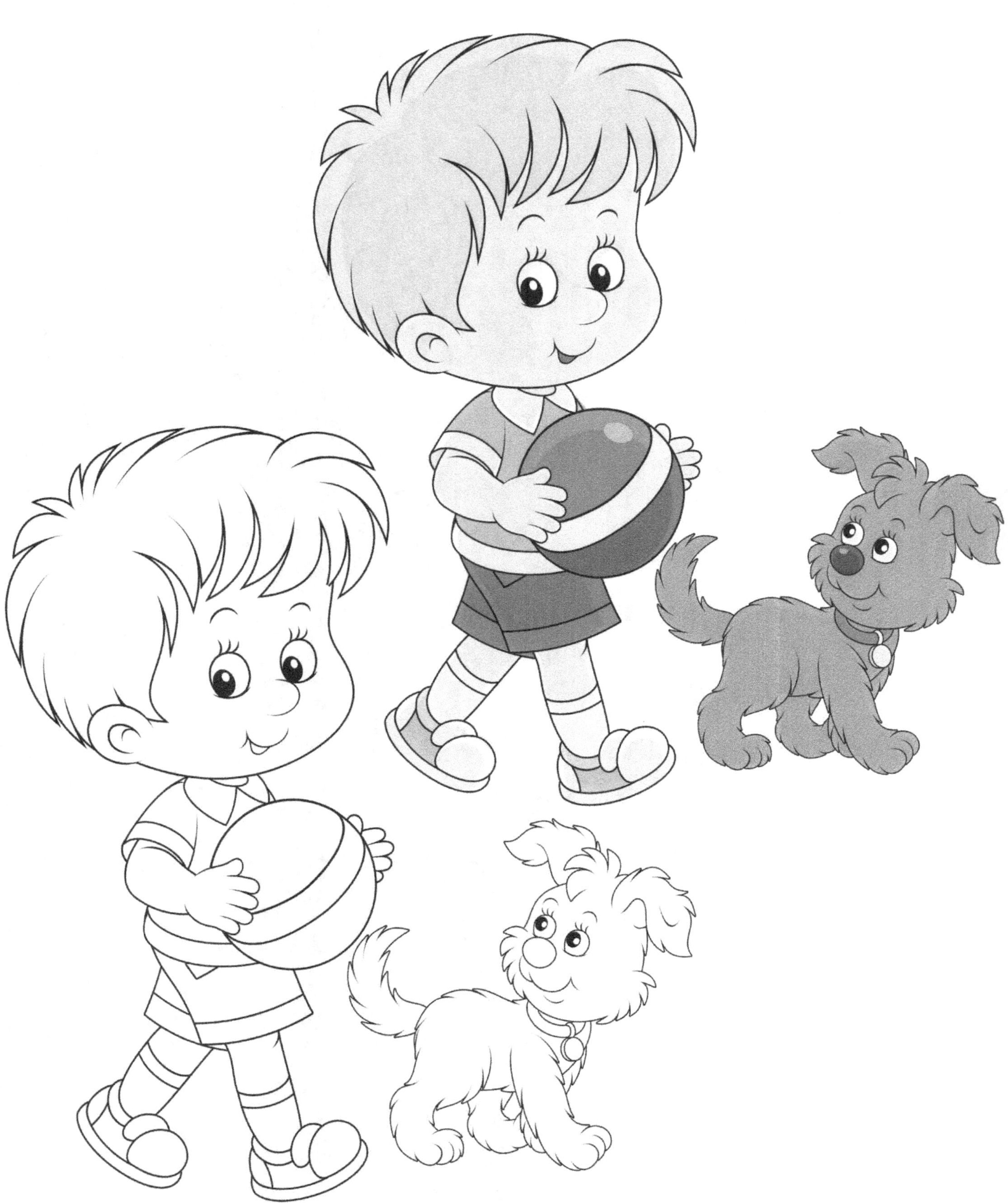

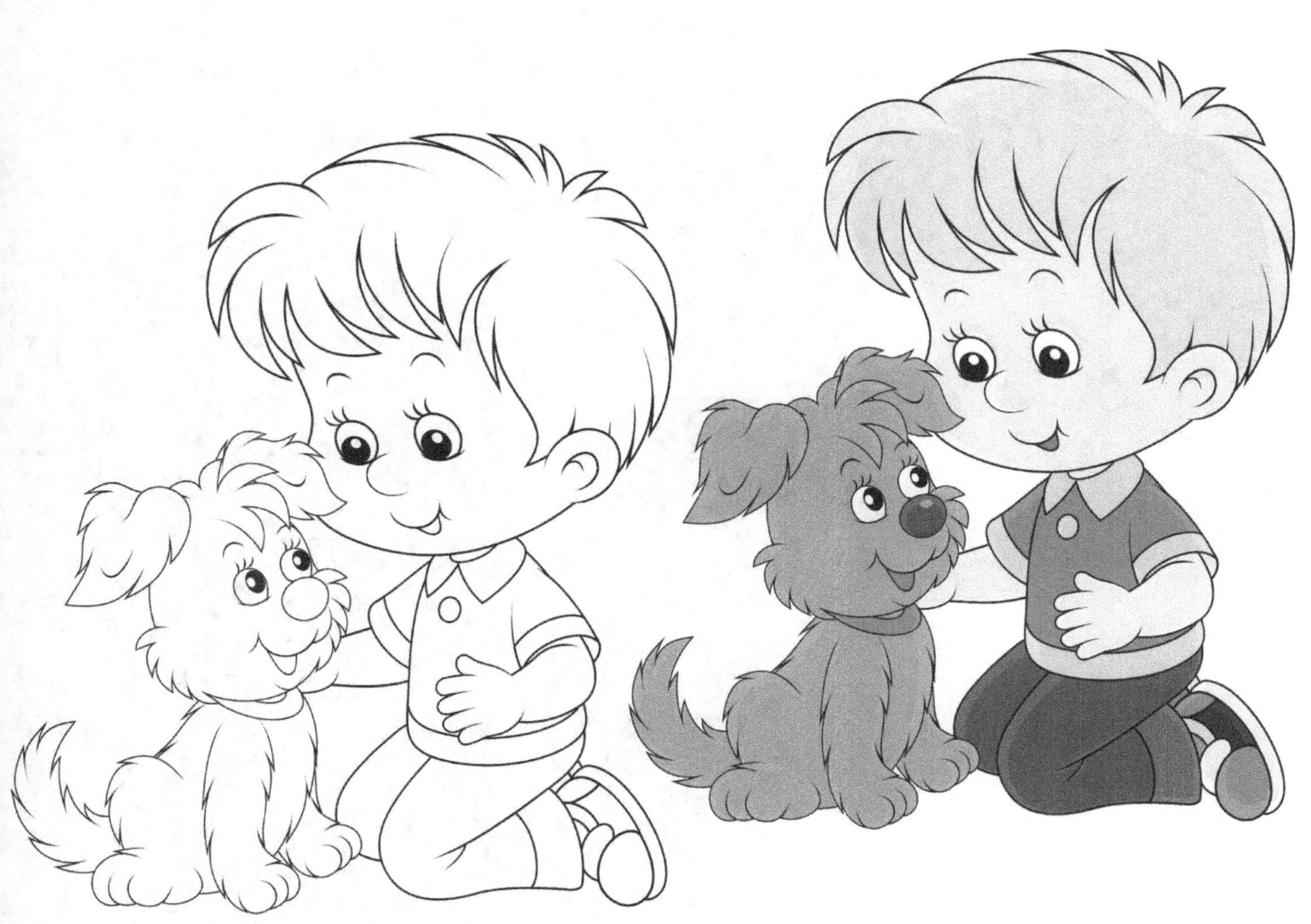

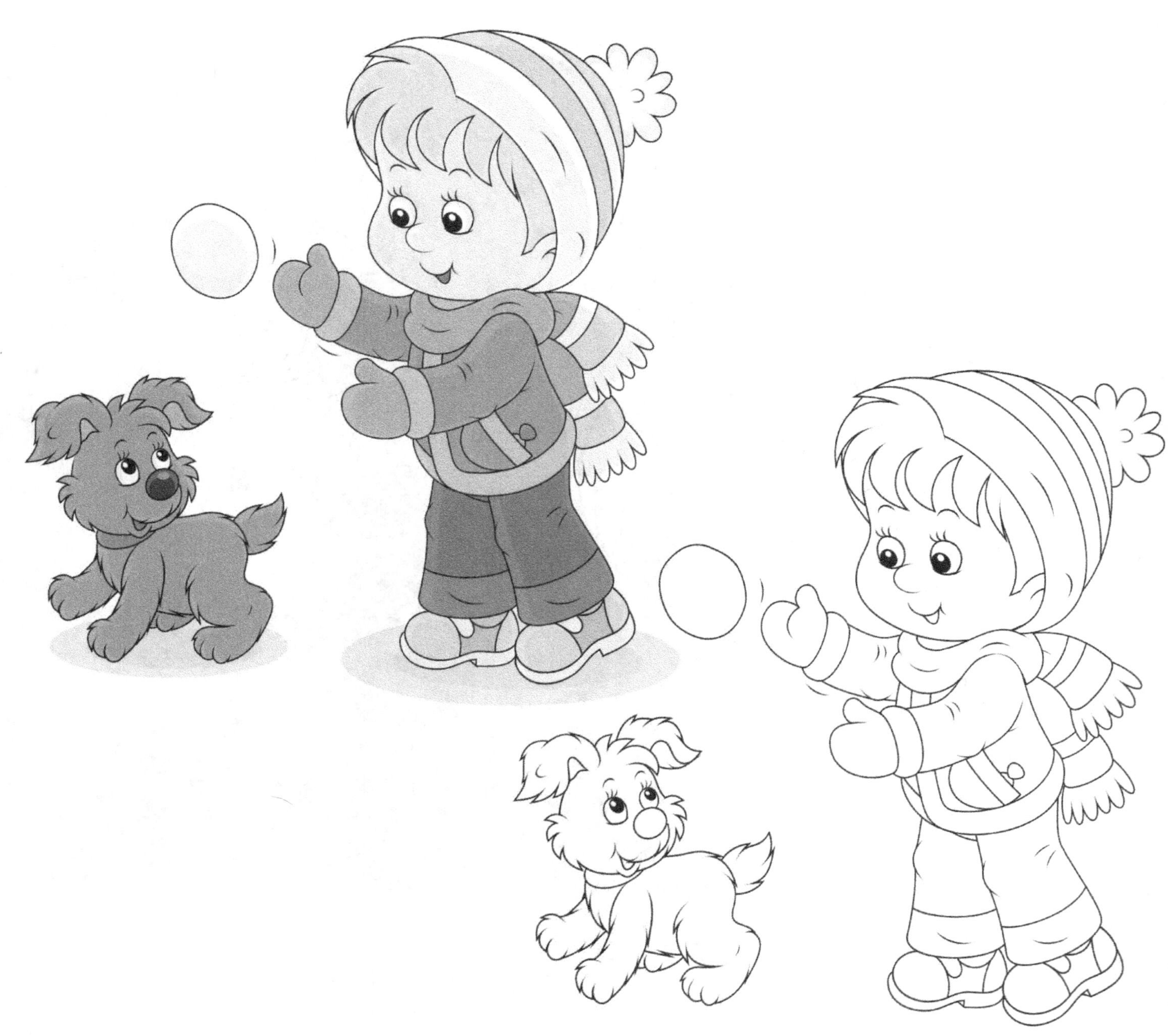

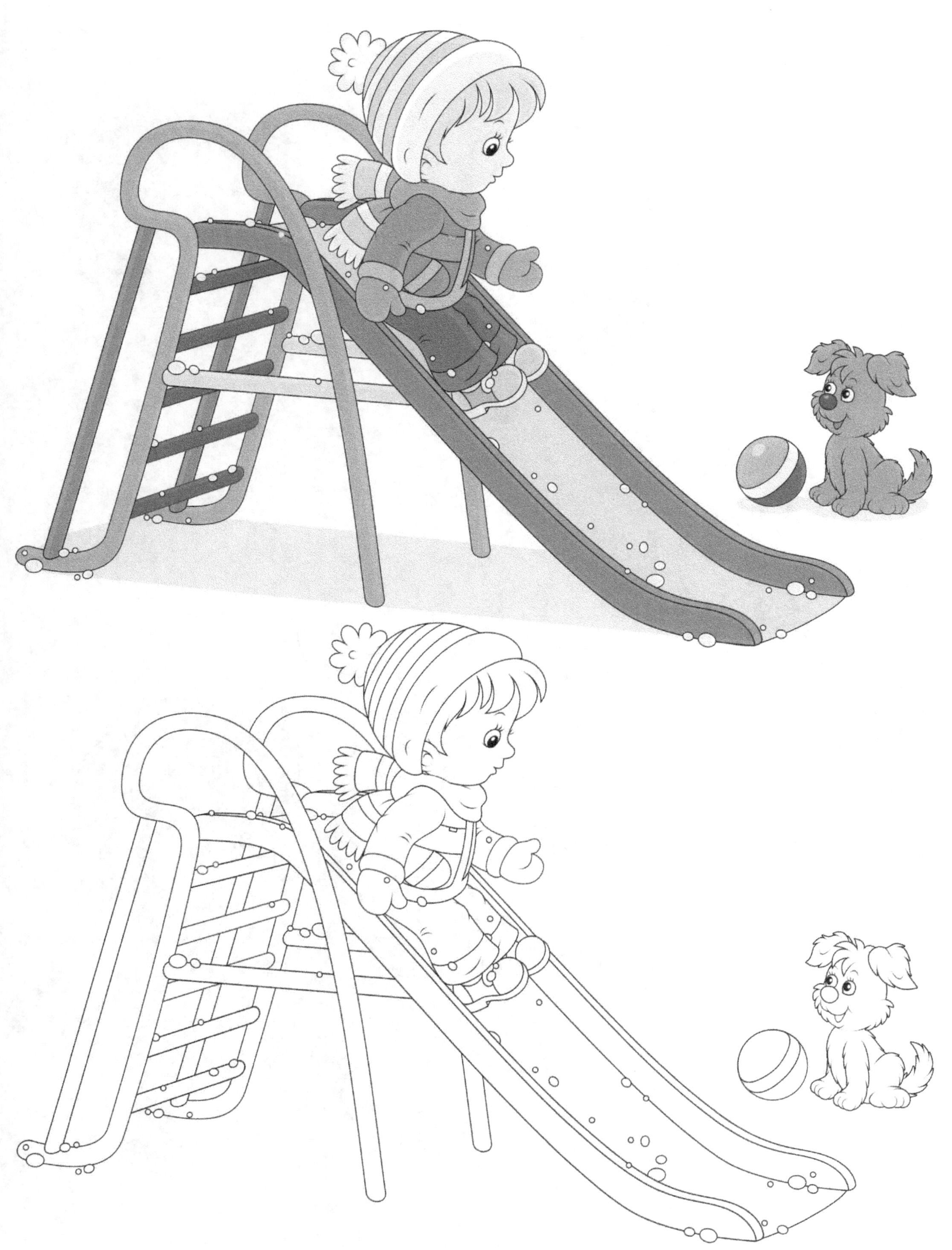

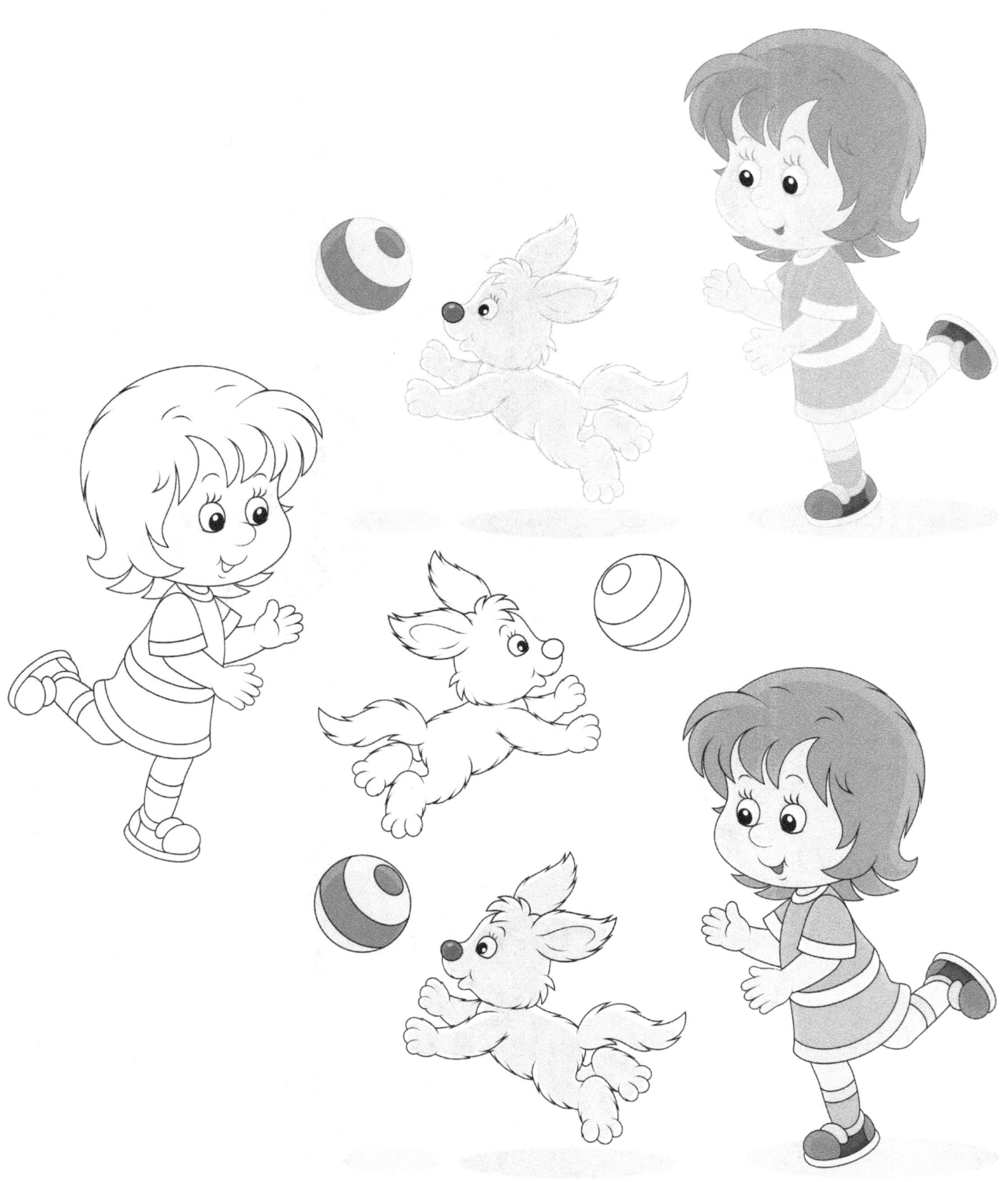

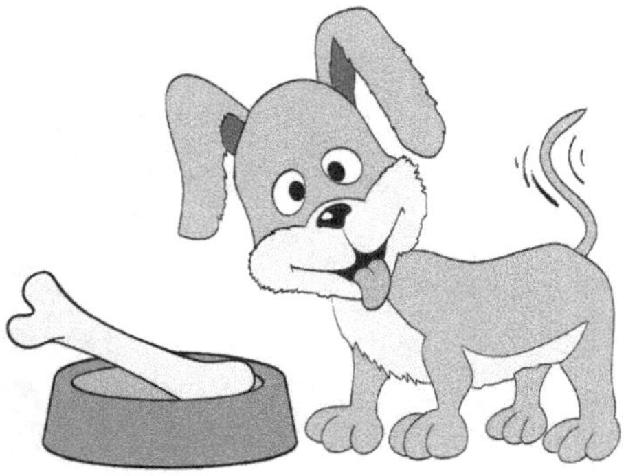

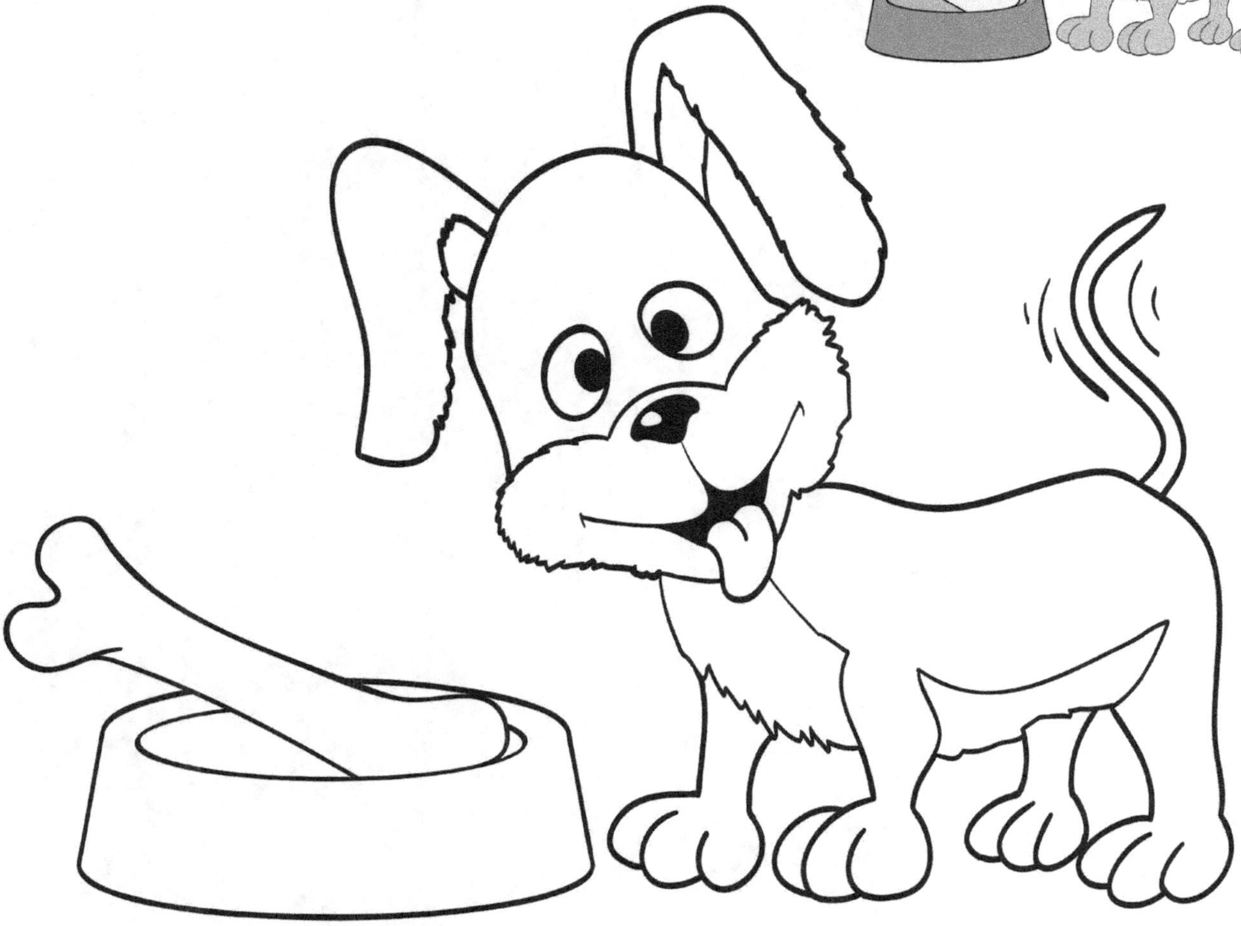